Chris Thorpe

THE MYSTERIES

T0353543

OBERON BOOKS
LONDON

WWW.OBERONBOOKS.COM

First published in 2018 by Oberon Books Ltd
521 Caledonian Road, London N7 9RH
Tel: +44 (0) 20 7607 3637 / Fax: +44 (0) 20 7607 3629
e-mail: info@oberonbooks.com
www.oberonbooks.com

PB ISBN: 9781786826312
E ISBN: 9781786826367

Cover image: 8bitnorthxstitch

10 9 8 7 6 5 4 3 2 1

Main Settings

Eskdale, Cumbria
Staindrop, County Durham
Whitby, North Yorkshire
Boston, Lincolnshire
Stoke-on-Trent, Staffordshire
Manchester, Greater Manchester

Characters

The same cast of six play the characters in each scene. The details of these characters change according to the scene's location. Characters in one scene are not aware of the existence of the other scenes or stories. In effect each scene takes place in its own world. In each scene, there are two strands of verse – one in meter, one rhythmically more free.

The Mysteries was first performed at Royal Exchange Theatre, Manchester on 25 October 2018 with the following cast:

Nigel Barrett	(GERRY)
Benjamin Cawley	(MARK)
Nadia Clifford	(GINNY)
Laurietta Essien	(MONA)
Hannah Ringham	(AMY)
Andrew Sheridan	(ANDY/ ANDRIUS)

WRITER	Chris Thorpe
DIRECTOR	Sam Pritchard
DESIGNER	Rosie Elnile
LIGHTING DESIGNER	Mark Distin-Webster
SOUND DESIGNER	Mike Winship
SOUND ASSOCIATE & TOURING TECHNICIAN	Gerry Marsden
ASSOCIATE DIRECTOR	Atri Banerjee
CASTING DIRECTOR	Jerry Knight-Smith CDG
TOURING PRODUCER	Kate Reynolds
STAGE MANAGER	Sarah Goodyear

Opening text

Hello.

Thanks for coming.

This is a show about all of us.

It's based in a specific community – maybe not that far from here. But this room – what goes on in it tonight – it isn't an impersonation of that community. We're not here to talk like you, walk like you, look like you. The people we're putting on stage aren't the specific people that exist out there. These are not their lives. But, the people we've invented have been nudged this way and that, given details and facts by the real people who live here.

We're not experts in what it's like here – you are. But we did talk to some people. We wandered around. Stayed over. Went to the pub. Joined in for a short while. We talked about politics. About who owns the land. About who comes in, who leaves. About the story a place tells itself so it can understand itself. About what a community needs – the facts that need to be shared so it can call itself a community. And one time, we did karaoke.

This is an attempt to show you a small part of what we saw, and why it feels important for us to try and understand this place, as part of the fabric of the bigger place we all live in.

Eskdale

Music. Aotearoa / God Defend New Zealand. A MAN enters, leading a sheep. He shears the sheep, quickly and efficiently. He leads the sheep offstage.

The Roman Fort at the western end of Hardknott Pass in Cumbria. Mid-morning. Late May.

AMY, with a camera. A woman in her late forties, wearing jeans and a jumper. She looks down the valley. She takes a photograph. GINNY, late teens.

GINNY: I can see your house from here.

AMY: Can you.

GINNY: This wall could do with a bit of work. How old do you think it is?

AMY: Dunno. Why don't you lick it and have a guess? I think that's how they do it on *Time Team.*

   …

   There's information boards, you know.

GINNY: All these men up here.

AMY: How many?

GINNY: Don't know.

AMY: I bet it says on the boards.

GINNY: All these men, probably doing all sorts.

   …

   What was this bit?

AMY: Bath house.

GINNY: Doing all sorts in the bath house. All that oil.

AMY: What oil?

GINNY: They brought it in stone jars. Landed it at Ravenglass.

AMY: How do you know that?

GINNY: Did that school project. Only time you refused to help me with my homework.

AMY: Did I?

GINNY: Yeah.

    …

They told us they used to sweat.

AMY: Long walk from Ravenglass.

GINNY: In the baths. They used to get clean by sweating.

AMY: They told you that at school?

GINNY: I suppose they thought we'd find it interesting.

AMY: About the oil?

GINNY: No. Well about the oil coming up here. Not about them oiling each other up.

AMY: Invented that yourself, did you? With your dirty little mind?

GINNY: It's hardly unlikely, is it? Given the Romans.

AMY: Given the Romans what?

GINNY: Had a famously open attitude to sexuality.

AMY: I haven't thought about that in years. You studying this place. When I was at school they never even brought us up here. Not that I remember, anyway. We never even really thought of it. Just up the road.

GINNY: Maybe if they'd brought you you'd have stayed.

AMY: I'm not sure a lack of school trips is what drove me away.

GINNY: Well. We're here now.

ANDY, in a pub in the valley. Note – the metre used for ANDY's verse in this section is modelled on the Wakefield Stanza from the Wakefield Mystery Plays.

ANDY: When light breaks, as it will and always has

Crests Eastern fells to spill along the pass

The shadows latched in ghylls begin to loose

And dark flees from the hills at daybreak's force

The fort begins

To rise from rocky ground

Find shape from formless mound

Its weathered walls around

To close us in

This first enclosure in a foreign land

Built to designs perfected far to south

Projecting power from Empire's outstretched hand

The boats drawn up at sandy river-mouth

Then, stone by stone

To guard the valley head

To claim where conquest led

To keep the soldiers fed

To stay, to own

And on the valley floor life carried on

The clearing trees, the creep of sheep and cow

The slow acceptance that one world was gone

A larger world connected with it now

Once sealed away

The trails of commerce grew

Cut by a wind that blew

And spliced and forged anew

Those roots that lay

There used to be poets here.

MONA: Fucking skype.

ANDY: Eh?

MONA: I fucking hate it.

ANDY: Who you trying to talk to?

MONA: Grant.

ANDY: Oh.

MONA: Fuck New Zealand.

ANDY: Delivery coming at ten.

MONA: It's unreasonably far away.

ANDY: Thirteen hours ahead.

MONA: Thirteen hours ahead.

ANDY: I'll just sort it on my own then, shall I?

MONA: Can you sort it on your own? I want to speak to him before he goes to bed.

ANDY: No problem.

MONA: I wish he hadn't gone back.

ANDY: Yeah.

...

There was a bit of frost on the top this morning.

MONA: Carrying it all. It's not good for me.

ANDY: Going to be a busy weekend.

MONA: She'll love it if I don't get to speak to him.

GERRY enters.

GERRY: I'm assuming you're open.

ANDY: Door's unlocked, so I guess we are. Semi-legal breakfast pint, Gerry?

GERRY: Tea.

ANDY: Working today?

GERRY: Aye.

ANDY: How's things at the plant?

GERRY: Progressing. Safely. And as cheaply as possible.

ANDY: Good to know you're spending my taxes wisely.

GERRY: I'm in no rush. Decommissioning's a slow process. Suits me fine. Longer I live here the happier I get. My plan is, by the time they run out of spent fuel rods, you'll have accepted me as one of your own.

MONA: You bought your house yeah, Gerry? I'm remembering that right?

GERRY: Yeah. Not going anywhere.

MONA: How much?

GERRY: How much what?

MONA: Did you buy it for?

GERRY: What the market said it was worth.

MONA: But how much, really?

GERRY: Why're you asking?

MONA: I'm not.

GERRY: You blatantly are.

MONA: Personal reasons.

GERRY: You want to know how much I paid for my house for personal reasons.

ANDY: I think what she's saying is –

MONA: You see one of the good things, Gerry, having people like you around, is you're a benchmark.

GERRY: Am I?

MONA: You come here, making property more expensive, you could at least tell us how expensive you're making it.

GERRY: Or you could ask an estate agent. I mean it doesn't really matter does it, what I paid for it. Because I think what you're asking is – what is it worth now?

ANDY: Never get a straight answer.

MONA: Never get a straight answer.

GERRY: It's not so much that I won't tell you. I just don't know. It's not something I check.

…

How's your brother?

MONA: I'm trying to find out.

ANDY: Why don't you go and give him another try? Nearly half-ten at night over there.

MONA: Yeah.

ANDY: Hasn't he got an early start?

MONA: Course he has.

MONA leaves.

GERRY: What was that about?

ANDY: My father's father's mother ran the post

As world and commerce thrust their tendrils through

The passes that had kept us cut from most

Of business, Empire, wars, their ebb and flow

She let it in

Through calls to work or war

Demands of nation, for

The rich to force the poor

To fight or spin

GINNY and AMY.

GINNY: Can we go back yet?

AMY: No.

GINNY: Give her a chance to calm down.

AMY: She doesn't need a chance to calm down.

GINNY: Could have fooled me.

GINNY picks something up from the floor.

Look at this.

AMY: What is it?

GINNY: Coin. Are we going to be rich?

AMY takes the coin from GINNY.

AMY: Very funny.

GINNY: Fifty pence. Still worth having.

AMY: Best spend it quick.

GINNY: Probably all sorts here though.

AMY: Been crawled over for years.

GINNY: Arrowheads.

AMY: I've seen enough arrowheads.

GINNY: Where?

AMY: Telly. Museums.

GINNY: Never see any planes, do you, here?

AMY: Course you do. They go right over.

GINNY: Not often though.

…

You ever stand in a spot and wonder about everything that's ever happened in it?

AMY: Can't say I do.

GINNY: All the other people that lived there. Or died there. Like if you could see time as a… shape. You could run a slider forwards and backwards.

…

See the walls come back up. Stone by stone.

AMY: I'd be more interested in pushing it forward a day or two.

GINNY: Nah. You can't see what hasn't happened til it's happened.

…

Pretty much anywhere you stand in this country you'd see someone die.

AMY: Morbid.

GINNY: Bet someone died right here.

AMY: Give it a rest eh, Gin?

GINNY: Some kid. Long way from home. Goes out to check on an outpost in the forest. It was probably all forest, wasn't it?

…

Staggers back with an arrow in his shoulder, or his head half-broken in. Dies right here. Where was he from?

AMY: They were from Dalmatia. Croatia.

GINNY: Look at you, knowing stuff.

AMY: Nothing wrong with that.

GINNY: Nothing wrong with that.

AMY: Just read the information board.

GINNY: Didn't you ever feel that, about history, growing up here?

AMY: Didn't you ever feel that, growing up in Manchester?

GINNY: That's not an answer.

AMY: Yes it is.

…

And no. I can't say I ever felt that. I didn't really think about history. I don't think you do, if it's the place you live.

GINNY: Not even here?

AMY: It's the kind of thing you think about in places you're just visiting. If a place is your everyday life you don't live in the past.

GINNY: Not even when you come back?

AMY: You live in your own past then, I reckon. Not the one that everyone agrees on.

GINNY: My fucking feet are killing me.

AMY: Shouldn't have come up here in new boots. I told you.

GINNY: It's not like I had any old boots to put on, is it?

The pub.

GERRY: You can see, can't you, how something like that could happen?

ANDY: Frankly, no.

GERRY: Look. All I'm saying is –

   …

   The sooner we get used to it the better.

MONA enters.

ANDY: You speak to him?

MONA: Yeah.

ANDY: Well then.

   …

   We should sort the cellar out.

MONA: The fucking bastard.

ANDY: Oh.

GERRY: What's up?

MONA: What's up is he doesn't give a shit is what's up/

GERRY: Is this your brother/

ANDY: So I'll get down there, shall/

MONA: Do what you fucking want, he says. What kind of a –

   …

   He'll just go along with whatever we want from however many fucking thousand miles away. Cheap enough to get on a plane and leave, but suddenly a bit expensive to pay your own airfare when it's time to come home and bury your dad. And then he says he'll go along with whatever we decide to do, as if he doesn't need the fucking money.

…

Fucking New Zealand. I hope the whole place falls into the sea.

GERRY: Well it's certainly –

…

It's seismically active. If that's helpful.

ANDY: So shall we do that, then? Sort the cellar out?

MONA: You would know that.

GERRY: It's kind of my job.

MONA: Fucking science. We never used to talk about science til you came in here Gerry. You've changed the character of the area.

GERRY: Fucking immigrants, eh. Coming here. Driving up the house prices.

…

You're welcome.

The fort.

AMY: Well.

GINNY: Ten more minutes.

AMY: No point putting it off.

GINNY: Isn't that why we came up here in the first place?

AMY: Maybe. But she'll be waiting.

GINNY: I don't need to be there.

AMY: I wish I didn't.

> *Pause.*

> Can you find your own way back?

> *The pub.*

ANDY: It used to be, so born, and so you are

> And that was happiness, or not, but there

> A life mapped out in function and in form

> And rarely moving from house, hall or farm

> But not so now

> We leave, and we return

> Or maybe bridges burn

> To trap us far from homes

> That once we knew

MONA: What the fuck are these?

ANDY: Free case of something they want to try out.

MONA: Apricot cider?

ANDY: I know.

MONA: Do they even know where they're sending this stuff?

ANDY: All just numbers isn't it? They want to see how it sells.

MONA: I think they're going to be unpleasantly surprised.

> …

> I'm not sure this place fits in the demographic for apricot cider. You can't really put a number on that. I just know it.

ANDY: You just wait til the summer. It'll fly out.

The fort.

GINNY: If this was a certain kind of play

There'd be a sound effect now

Something so subtle, you'd hardly notice it –

Sub-bass vibrating on the edge of perception

And the lights would shift, again

Not so much you'd be aware, not consciously

But you'd know something in this reality had changed

And unseen by me, somewhere over there

Behind my shoulder, like a magic trick

Would appear a young man

Armoured like a Roman auxiliary

Or as accurately as the designer could manage

While still providing freedom of movement

And we would be, suddenly, in

A Space Outside Of Time

(I hope you heard the capital letters when I said that)

And I would be surprised, shocked, even

But not so shocked as to be dramatically

Inconvenient, and then me, and

This young man from two thousand years ago

Each one thinking the other was a ghost

Would hesitate, like animals walking

For the first time past a mirror

And after a few false starts, we would talk,

Each one knowing the other's language

Without the need for lengthy explanation

You would just accept that because

This place is whatever it says it is

And we trust you not to poke

Unnecessary holes

And from our conversation, we would learn

By 'we' I mean the people in this room

That something connects us across time

And there are parallel longings

And none of this is new, or even real,

And –

MARK appears behind GINNY. He works on a farm in the valley. He is in his early twenties.

MARK: Haven't seen a sheep have you?

GINNY: What the fuck?

MARK: About this tall? Answers to the name of –

...

I'm just kidding. We don't name them. Although you'd be surprised how many people think we do.

Pause.

GINNY: Sorry. No.

MARK: Ah, no bother. I thought I saw one of ours from the road. It'll turn up. They usually do. Had a call on the way over to keep my eye out. Someone spotted one of ours up here where it shouldn't be.

   …

Sometimes one'll wander off. Forget it's hefted. Probably not even ours.

   …

Don't worry.

GINNY: I wasn't, til you told me not to.

MARK: I'm not.

   …

Just meant, carry on with whatever it was you were doing.

GINNY: Right. I'll do that, then. I'll just do that.

MARK: OK.

GINNY: OK.

MARK: Archaeology. Is it?

GINNY: What?

MARK: Some kind of project? Roman stuff. Don't come up here much.

GINNY: No. I'm just visiting.

MARK: I live here.

GINNY: You're lucky.

MARK: I am.

Pause.

Are you waiting for someone?

GINNY: No. I was just going to head back down.

MARK: That's a coincidence, me too.

The pub. AMY enters. GERRY is still drinking his tea.

GERRY: I can give them a shout if you want.

AMY: No, it's OK.

GERRY: If you want a drink. They're down in the cellar, I think.

…

You alright?

AMY: Fine. Yes. Thanks. I'll wait.

GERRY: Things tend to take their time. Round here.

AMY: Sure.

GERRY: When it's quiet at least.

…

Come the weekend, this time of year. Won't be able to move in here. Wouldn't see me here at the weekend. I'll be at home with a film on and a few bottles of something. Andy'll be rushed off his feet. Exhausted. Won't be a spare seat. All dogs and walking boots.

…

No place for locals, this, on a weekend in spring. No offence.

AMY: What?

GERRY: No offence. I didn't mean that people who aren't –

    …

    You're very welcome. Here.

AMY: Well. Thanks.

GERRY: Beautiful isn't it?

AMY: I hadn't really –

GERRY: I sometimes just –

    …

    I mean. To walk out of your front door, and see all. This.
    That. Out there. It's not something –

    …

    I mean, I don't know where you come from, but it's not
    something you ever get tired of, you know? Maybe you
    do. Maybe you do know. Or you've been here before.

    …

    People do that, obviously. Come back over and over
    again. And I think. To them, that must feel like a little like
    living here. In a way. And who knows, maybe it does. But
    you don't see many of them here in the winter. They'll not
    come then. Funny that. Feels like they want to live here,
    but not really *live* here, you know.

    …

    Winter can be. I mean, it's cruel. But wonderful. The quiet.

AMY: You must have some stories.

GERRY: Once there was a guy. One of the old guys, this was.
    Before any of this. When it was properly wild up here.
    Not all these holiday homes. There was a winter in. The

forties, I think. Cold came in and it was like it was never
going to go away. I wasn't round of course. Before my –

...

Ran a farm up the valley, he did. About a mile away.
Farm house is still there. Hard as nails. Of course that's a
given round here. Anyway he's up the valley, other side
of the Esk – that's the river – just below the crags, fixing a
wall. Now the weather here, it can come on suddenly. You
should watch that, by the way. Even on a day like this, you
can be walking along happy as Larry and a few minutes
later, can't even see your feet. So suddenly this blizzard
blows up from nowhere, and this old guy. Young guy then,
of course. Long dead now. But this guy decides, discretion,
valour and all that, he's going to get home. Thing is though,
up here, it can dump a foot of snow on you in fifteen
minutes. Less. So, he's making his way down to what he
thinks is the path. And of course round here you have to
know the country like the back of your hand, and he did.
But that winter was. Well it was something exceptional.
And he loses his way, and next thing he knows he's falling.
Rolling and falling like he's never going to stop. Not
panicking. These old guys. You see it round here still. Never
seen one panic. But try as he might he can't stop himself.
Somewhere in all that tumbling, he hits his head on a rock.
You might notice them all lying about here. Relic of the ice-
age, they are. But anyway, wakes up hours later, how many,
he can't tell, but it's gone dark. Still snowing, but he can
hear the river. Freezing cold, but all he's lost is a glove. He
follows the river downstream. Obviously with a reference
point he can make it back to the house. Checks the sheep.
Gets in, lights the lantern. Realises losing the glove means
his hand's been exposed to the cold for God knows how
long. Fingers, all black. No feeling in them. Of course today
you'd be straight off to the hospital, but he knows there's
no chance of that. Couldn't even get to a doctor, assuming

there was one in Boot at the time, which I'm not sure there was. You can't imagine, can you, in the modern world, being that cut off? Nearly got run over by an ASDA van the other day. So his fingers all black. No feeling. Dead, basically. What does he do?

AMY: What does he do?

GERRY: Hatchet. Kitchen table. Off they come. One swing, clean cut. Bandages his hand. Doesn't even think to mention it unless people ask him what happened. Just gets on with his life. And that's the way it is.

AMY: Wow.

GERRY: I know. And that's not even … round here, that kind of story. Not exceptional.

AMY: What was his name?

GERRY: His name?

AMY: The farmer?

GERRY: Now let's –

    …

    Like I say. Before my time. I think it was –

AMY: Tommy Barnes.

GERRY: Tommy Barnes.

AMY: His name was Tommy Barnes. He was my grandad's brother.

GERRY: Oh.

AMY: Nineteen forty-seven, by the way. January forty-seven. If you want to tell the story better next time. Coldest winter in memory up here at that point. Although sixty-two was colder. Coldest one for the rest of time, suppose sixty-two might end up, the way things are going. You could incorporate that too, as a detail. For the tourists.

…

Or keep it the way it is. Doesn't bother me. It was a good story. I liked it.

Pause.

Work at the old power station do you? Reprocessing?

GERRY: Decommissioning. I'm an engineer.

AMY: How long have you lived here?

GERRY: A year. Just over.

AMY: Good for you.

…

I'm glad you made it through one winter. Good luck for the next one.

GERRY: Can I get you a drink?

AMY: It'll be on the house if I want one. Don't worry yourself.

MONA walks in with a crate of bottled lager.

ANDY: The tiniest of places sows its seeds

And some of them blow out into the world

But keep their roots deep-threaded, and their needs

Though stretched by time, still touch with tips unfurled

Remembered hearts

They feel the pull, the call

Of memory, in thrall

To silent ranks of all

They tore apart

Just below the fort. GINNY and MARK are on the way down the valley.

GINNY: My ears just popped.

MARK: It's the quiet. Still does it to me, sometimes.

GINNY: What's that?

MARK: What's what?

GINNY: That bird there.

MARK: Buzzard.

GINNY: What's it doing?

MARK: Looking for something to eat.

GINNY: Is that it?

MARK: What do you think birds do apart from that?

GINNY: Make other birds.

MARK: That's pretty much it.

GINNY: Fair enough. Can't say I'm not disappointed though.

MARK: What by?

GINNY: Your lack of seductive rustic knowledge. I kind of thought you were going to start telling me about the mysteries of nature.

MARK: The mysteries of sheep I can do. It's basically sheep or nothing.

GINNY: Tell me about the mystery of sheep.

MARK: The main mystery is why we still bother.

GINNY: Which one's yours?

MARK: Can't see our place from here. Isn't really ours, anyway. National Trust's really. Though I doubt they'd take it off us.

GINNY: Would you barricade yourselves in?

MARK: No. We're just good.

GINNY: Spinning wool into gold.

MARK: Hardly. Shear eight hundred sheep in four days, you hardly make enough money to pay the electric bill for the clippers.

   …

You know there's no money around here.

GINNY: And I thought I'd met a rich landowner.

MARK: And I thought I'd met a rich student.

GINNY: What makes you think I'm a student?

MARK: Just a guess.

GINNY: Well you're wrong.

MARK: What makes you think we own the land?

   …

Have a look out there. What are we looking at?

GINNY: Well that's a buzzard. I've learned that much.

MARK: The bit underneath the buzzard. Who owns it?

GINNY: Tell me.

MARK: You. It's what this country would look like with the top bit stripped off. The bit that's parcelled up into private ownership and interests and the right to make money off it. Used to be there were landowners here. Hasn't been true for years. Not really, anyway. It was common land, then it was parcelled up. Then it was sold off. Then it was bought back. Now you own it.

GINNY: Me?

MARK: Or rather, it's owned on your behalf. The country owns it.

GINNY: So it's still owned.

MARK: Better than the alternative.

GINNY: Which is?

MARK: Private landlords and conference centres as far as the fucking eye can see. Some millionaire prick with his own helicopter and a newspaper to run. Or maybe they're community-minded. Revitalisation. Same helipad but the helicopter runs on soya milk. Or an investment group based in some Chinese city you've never heard of.

GINNY: You don't want to own it?

MARK: Couldn't make a living, doing what we do.

GINNY: I'll have to tell my mum she owns all this. It'll make her feel better.

MARK: On holiday with your mum, are you?

GINNY: I didn't say I was on holiday.

...

So why are you doing it? What you do?

24

MARK: Because some things shouldn't just be about the money.

GINNY: So they should be about what?

   …

The look of it? Are you just doing this so I can come here and look at you?

The pub.

MONA: Where's the kid?

AMY: Following me down. She's not/

MONA: Not a kid, I know, but –

   …

Always think of some people that way, don't you?

ANDY: Any particular thing you want to drink, Amy?

MONA: I'll get it.

AMY: Haven't said what I want yet.

MONA: I'll get it. I know what she wants.

MONA gets AMY a glass of wine, and pours one for herself.

AMY: It's a bit early.

MONA: Nobody gives a shit.

   …

Have you met Gerry?

AMY: We were just chatting.

GERRY: Never knew you had relatives.

MONA: We're not related.

AMY: Sisters.

MONA: Have to have a relationship to be related.

AMY: Gerry was telling me about Uncle Tommy.

MONA: Old hatchet-hand.

GERRY: Obviously if I'd known I was telling you –

AMY: It's nice you know the story. If they're telling you stories
    in a place. Means you belong, I suppose.

ANDY: It's good to see you, Amy/

MONA: Been up to the church this morning?

ANDY: I understand you're staying/

MONA: She's down in Boot.

AMY: In a holiday let.

ANDY: Lucky to get one of those, this time of year.

AMY: Weekdays weren't so busy. We'll be gone before the
    weekend.

ANDY: Want some crisps?

MONA: Does she look like she wants some fucking crisps,
    Andy?

Pause.

AMY: I'll be alright.

Pause.

ANDY: You still doing the –

    …

    What was it?

26

AMY: Council. Manchester.

ANDY: Yeah. That was it. All good, is it? They keeping you busy?

AMY: Yeah. For now.

ANDY: Good. Well. Got some time off work then.

...

Good.

Below the fort. Further down the valley.

MARK: Where you headed?

GINNY: Pub.

MARK: Meeting someone?

GINNY: My mum, and my auntie.

MARK: You in any hurry?

GINNY: Christ, no.

MARK: Let me show you something first.

GINNY: What?

MARK: Further down the valley. It's past the pub. My car's just at the bottom here though. I can drive us.

GINNY: Are you a safe driver?

MARK: Trust me. I'm a local.

The pub.

ANDY: From time to time a death will bring us back

Although we know the links have lost their power

We know this in our bones as well – the lack

Of thought to history hour to hour

Does not translate

Into its vanishing

It stays, a living thing

Unseen, but poised to spring

Its hand on fate

By the River Esk. St Catherine's Church. The churchyard.

GINNY: Peaceful.

MARK: It's the river. Gives it an aura.

GINNY: You think I've got a thing for graveyards?

MARK: No.

GINNY: Meet a strange woman up a mountain, and you think. I know. I'll take her to a graveyard.

MARK: Just thought you might like to see it.

GINNY: Based on what?

MARK: Relic. Same as the fort. Dead. But of historical interest to the visitor.

GINNY: Looks pretty alive to me. There's a notice over there for a coffee morning. Didn't see one of them at the fort. Guess the Romans aren't having many coffee mornings these days.

MARK: Oh yeah. I mean it's still. Still a working church and that.

GINNY: People still get buried here?

MARK: Not many.

GINNY: When was the last time you came here?

MARK: Your grandad's funeral.

Pause.

GINNY: How the fuck do you know who my grandad is?

MARK: You're Mona's niece.

GINNY: News travels fast.

MARK: Wasn't hard to work out. But yeah. Knew already.

GINNY: Why didn't you say?

…

You know what? I don't care. Not my business.

MARK: You want to see where he's buried?

GINNY: I guess. I never knew him, really.

Pause.

MARK: People seemed to like him. Not one for talking though. Never really mentioned your mum.

GINNY: She never mentioned him either. I think they just didn't get on. Or maybe she just didn't get on with this place.

MARK: Why are you here?

GINNY: Didn't want Mum driving up from Manchester on her own.

MARK: Which way did you come?

GINNY gestures.

GINNY: Over the top. Kind of that way.

MARK: Birker Moor. Lots of slate up there. Eskdale's granite. Beckstone in Wasdale.

GINNY: All looks the same to me.

MARK: No it doesn't. You think it does, but it doesn't. If I put all those three things on the ground in front of you now, you'd see they were different.

GINNY: Would it matter?

MARK: Not really, unless you were building a wall out of it. Or tunnelling into it. They might do that. Need somewhere to put the low-level waste from the reprocessing plant.

GINNY: Really?

MARK: It's got to go somewhere.

GINNY: But here?

MARK: Could be under us right now and you wouldn't notice.

Pause.

Did you know you were from here? When you were a kid?

GINNY: No. Don't think so. Mum never really mentioned it.

…

I mean it's not like she deliberately hid it. It's just she never mentioned it. I think as soon as she got pregnant with me, she was gone.

MARK: Sure you don't want to see the grave?

GINNY: Plenty of graves here. It'd just be one more. I know you think this might be something special, but I never really missed it.

…

How come they haven't run out of space?

MARK: Not many folk get buried round here these days.

GINNY: How about you?

MARK: Hadn't thought about it, really.

GINNY: Course you have. You. Lying under the earth here, after a good life. Looking up at all this rock. Sound of the water.

MARK: Things change.

GINNY: There's a revelation isn't there?

You can feel it coming

Because this is how these stories end

The outsiders come in and

De-stabilise the status quo, they

Have to, that's their function

And things long drowned, or

Thought-drowned, get pulled

Into the light, gleaming like

That ancient Roman sword

We might have seen earlier

If it had been the ghost we expected

And not some young shepherd

Looking for a sheep, who is

Probably symbolic in his own way.

But this feels like the age-old story

Of someone coming back, and

A secret history, and perhaps

Disputed parentage, and we use

The small humanity of this place

In number, if not in scope

To map our own struggles

GINNY: So you won't be buried here?

MARK: If you mean here, as in, where we're standing. Who
knows?

…

If you mean, in the valley. If you mean, 'are you going
to leave'. Well I don't know that either. I've got some
romantic fucking idea about being buried here. But then
there used to be four schools, and now there's only one.
I don't mean anything by that. It's just a fact. About the
chances of staying.

…

There's a trade-off here. Between staying, and stewarding,
and never really owning it. Used to be different. A
thousand years ago, maybe. The time between the
Romans and the fences. You might not have had to worry
so much about who owned what. But now you do. And
you have to keep promises. And that's a good thing and a
bad thing.

GINNY: I wouldn't want to die here.

MARK: You might, if you'd grown up here.

…

I'm not gonna try and convince you because you didn't.
But you might.

The pub. AMY and MONA.

MONA: Is that it?

...

Seriously?

AMY: I don't know what else you want me to say.

Long pause.

How was he?

MONA: How was he?

AMY: At the end.

MONA: He was alive, and then he was fucking dead, Amy.

AMY: But was it –

MONA: Does it matter? He was alive and then he stopped being alive. Whether he was in pain, or smiling, or screaming is totally fucking irrelevant to the fact that he was alive and then he stopped being alive, and I'm not particularly interested in telling you what it was like. If you want to know what it was like, you should have fucking turned up yourself, don't you think?

AMY: Would have upset him.

MONA: We don't know that, do we, and now we never will.

...

Alright. Just before he died, he sat up in bed, and he looked around the room. And he said, where's Amy?

AMY: Oh fuck off.

MONA: No, seriously, he did. He opened his eyes, and he said, where's Amy, and I said, she's not here Dad, and he fucking cried out to heaven, oh why has my youngest daughter so cruelly decided to be absent in this, my final struggle, and a single tear fell on the pure white bed-sheets, and then he lay back and breathed his last, and the fucking curtains fluttered in a sudden breeze as his soul ascended into heaven.

…

Seriously. That's exactly how it went.

AMY: There was no need for that. No need.

MONA: Amy. He got very ill, and he was in a lot of pain, and they gave him drugs, and the drugs made the pain bearable, and then he fell asleep, and a bit after that he went from being asleep to being dead, and then he was dead and we buried him. Is that better?

AMY: Is that what happened?

MONA: Yes, that's what happened.

…

And he didn't mention you once.

Pause.

AMY: Well that's. That's fine. I wouldn't have expected –

…

I wouldn't have expected him to.

MONA: Still. Left you half the house, didn't he? Whether that's by accident or design is another mystery for the fucking ages. I want to get out of here.

AMY: I know.

MONA: So let me get out of here.

The churchyard.

GINNY: I should go.

MARK: I'm not stopping you.

Pause.

You don't actually want to though, do you?

GINNY: Haven't you got stuff to do?

…

Were you really looking for a sheep up there?

MARK: God's honest truth. Didn't recognise you until you turned round.

…

You've got your auntie's way of standing.

GINNY: That's romantic bullshit. I don't know her.

MARK: You don't have to. Sometimes your body just knows things and you don't really get a say in the matter. Could have stolen you from here as a baby, brought you up in some flat with no green in sight and something in you would still know.

GINNY: Well you got the bit about the flat right.

MARK: When you're that age, adults just want what they want, and you don't get a say in it.

GINNY: Oh I'm not complaining. I like being from where I'm from. Even if I stand like my auntie, I'm not from here.

MARK: It's all romantic bullshit, really.

…

Whatever story you tell yourself.

…

What do you think I am? What's my job?

GINNY: You're a shepherd.

MARK: Well, yeah. Partly. And what does that mean? I'm
one of a dying breed. I'm self-reliant. I'm a storehouse
of old skills, handed down over centuries. At one with
the landscape. You see this – all this – takes your breath
away, doesn't it? The green and the grey and the blue, if
you're lucky. The deep ghylls carved by pure water and
the glacial valleys and the crags standing over it all as if
they're guarding us from a hostile world. It's thrilling.
And I see something else. All this lovely topography
is a different thing to me, isn't it? I can read it in a
different way, because I'm part of it. I'm melded with
it. Psychically. I can read its moods. I can predict the
weather, and see the future in the light playing across a
scree slope. I can walk across the common land barefoot,
blindfold and tell you the direction of every summit
without thinking. I can deduce the result of elections from
rabbit shit. And so could my father, and his father, and his
father. And the women too, of course. Although they're
a different kind of touch. They're the ones who actually
keep the community together. And everyone knows
everyone. And because of that we're different.

…

Bollocks.

GINNY: Well, none of that's really true. I'll give you that. But
people need to believe it's true. You're playing your part
in the pretence.

MARK: Yeah. And that's my job, really. The sheep are just
incidental.

…

I want to tell you something. You mum's in the pub, right now. And I know what she's doing. She's trying to get a little piece of this. Because she thinks things are different here. That all that, what I've just said, is true. And it isn't. Whatever sense of connection she's looking for. It's just not there.

GINNY: She's not daft.

MARK: I know she's not daft. But there isn't any difference between here, and where she is now. Not really. Not in the way she wants there to be.

…

That connection doesn't really exist. All there is, is a process of coping with economic reality. Especially these days. This used to be a working landscape, and then it became this beautiful thing we wanted to preserve. And all I am is part of the machine that keeps that going.

GINNY: So why stay?

MARK: Why stay anywhere? I guess I like it. This is just my version of all the national pretending.

ANDY: The land was free, then common, farmed, enclosed

For benefit of those that owned the stocks

And later, when the riches the few forced

By taking tribute from the hill-fed flocks

Began to wane

The nation turned its gaze

To hills where poets blazed

Romantic, and amazed

It took their strain

Some forest planted, but the most part left

To sheep and shepherds, stewards of the fold

And if the valley's life was now bereft

Of ways to transmute gathered wool to gold

The country paid

The gain was worth the price

To fix here this device

To preserve paradise

Elsewhere unmade

The stark and bounding hills seal in belief

The villaged valleys here preserve a core

Allow a nation to convince itself

It holds dear values from a time before

We hold that truth

Although it is not true

We cling so tightly to

A heart we never knew

Like long lost youth

The pub.

MONA: You should go home.

…

Just go home, I'll sell up, you wait for the money to arrive.

AMY: I don't need the money.

MONA: I fucking do.

AMY: You've got the house to live in. All paid up.

MONA: I don't fucking want it.

AMY: Where would you go?

Pause.

MONA: Tell me what you want from me, Amy.

AMY: A place to stay.

…

Doesn't have to be forever.

MONA: It doesn't have to be here.

AMY: I'll buy you out.

MONA: How long will that take?

AMY: Give me a year.

MONA: A fucking year?

AMY: Maybe less.

MONA: And until then?

AMY: I could live with you.

MONA: Right.

AMY: I mean. It'd help me get the money together if –

MONA: Oh here we go.

Pause.

I'm selling the house, Amy. Whatever you think you want here, you won't get it. I'm selling the house and I'm giving you your part of the money and you can do what you want with it. But I'm not waiting around.

AMY: You can't sell it unless I say so.

MONA: Are you going to stop me?

…

Thought not. And I'm not waiting around.

AMY: I don't see what's so wrong. You're part of a community –

MONA: I serve pints of bitter to tourists. That's what I do. You think this place survives on the dominoes nights in the winter?

…

I serve pints of bitter to tourists and I clean rooms in bed and breakfasts. Don't get me wrong. I've got nothing against them. We'd be fucked without them. But it's what keeps this landscape going Amy. People being paid to do things the old way, and people paying to come and look at what happens when you pay people to do things the old way.

AMY: But if you let me buy you out –

MONA: I'm not waiting around for that to happen. It's time I went.

AMY: Six months then. I can get a plan together –

MONA: What plan?

AMY: This place is more connected than you realise. Look. If
I set up a consultancy. Work from home. I've got a lot of
transferable skills that –

…

Your half of whatever the house sells for. It isn't going to
go far anyway.

MONA: It'll go far enough. I don't need much.

AMY: I'll even pay over the odds.

MONA: It's not that it's just time for me to go, Amy. I think
you're looking for the wrong things here. The blood
connection. That's changed. It's changed because this
place isn't about family any more. It's about what this
country needs to preserve.

…

You won't find the right sort of home here. I'm saving you
from yourself.

AMY: This is my home.

MONA: It's not your home Amy. You had to make a decision
a long time ago, and you left to have a baby somewhere
else, when you could have stayed. We could have looked
after you. It's not your home. It just hasn't worked out
in the home you made and you've decided those old
connections mean something when they don't.

…

If things go downhill, this part of the country's going to
get sold off. Maybe not soon. But eventually. Let me sell
up quick to someone I don't care about. Someone I don't

give a shit about them being here when that happens. Or someone who doesn't care. Gerry. There's a bunch of people like him waiting. Let them take it over and install broadband and do surveys for nuclear storage. Let them keep coming to marvel at the unspoiled landscape.

GINNY enters with MARK.

AMY: I wish I had a good reason for you.

…

I wish this place wasn't so important. I wish I didn't look at you and know in my bones that we're related. I wish this didn't feel like it was anything to do with my life. But it does. Everything here feels real in a way that Manchester doesn't.

MONA: You should have come back sooner. Maybe you'd still have strong enough roots.

AMY: It took me thirty years to realise.

MONA: Well you should have stayed.

AMY: You could teach me, if I came back. How to be from here again.

MONA: How about this.

…

Why don't we sell the house, and I'll come live with you for a while.

…

You could teach me how to leave.

Pause.

GINNY: Hey, auntie Mona.

MONA: Where'd you find him?

GINNY: He's been showing me around.

MARK: Alright, Mona.

MONA: What the fuck are you doing, Mark?

MARK: Looking for a sheep. Got distracted.

GINNY: You alright, Mum?

MONA: It's not summer yet, Mark.

MARK: No it isn't.

MONA: Bit early in the year for a holiday romance.

MARK: Don't know what you're on about.

GINNY: Did you two get it sorted?

AMY: We're talking about it.

Pause.

MONA: You probably need to be heading off soon.

GINNY: We booked the cottage til tomorrow.

MONA: Well, it's a free country.

ANDY: That push and pull is never really done

　　Not just in families, but country-wide

　　The need to hold belief that we came from

　　Some soil-connected principle, take pride

　　From where we sprang

　　So chaos can have birth

　　From something of true worth

While money girds the Earth

Pretend we sang

Some age-old song of ground and nature once,

That still sounds faintly in the sharp-fanged mist

Of sovereignty or capital – romance

An origin where one did not exist

We freeze our fear

Of rootlessness, close-trapped

Beneath our mountains, capped

To shield us from lives mapped

On empty air

Pause. An awkward moment. Almost as if ANDY had suddenly said this in the reality of the pub. A decision to continue.

GERRY: Nothing's very far away from anything, is it, in this country? Not really. Take where I grew up. You'd think it was a million miles from here, but it isn't.

…

And it's not that different either. I like to think it is. But it's all connected.

…

It's not like I own any of this. I mean, I do. I own my house, because I could afford it. And I could afford it because I came from somewhere else. But then, I came from somewhere else because this place isn't too far away, and there's a job to do. We have to keep the lights on. So as I said, it's all connected.

…

You know what I feel when I walk out of my door, some mornings? Before I get in the car and drive to work. I feel blessed. I feel so blessed that all this is here, and the sun on the mountain slopes moves like honey and there's a nuclear power plant less than an hour's drive away where I can use my engineering degree. I feel like this needs to be here. Or what the hell is everything else for? It needs to be preserved, because at the heart of anywhere we live, there should be community. There should be interdependence. And that's laid bare here. That's the phrase. Laid bare. We need it as a living example just as much as we need electricity. We need to remember it should be at the heart of everything we do, because it's easy to forget. It's easy to forget there need to be bones in a body, until you're lucky enough to come to a place you can see the bones.

…

Of course that's how it has to feel. It has to look like that and feel like that. Even if it's just a pretend-version of how it used to be. Even if the rest of us have to prop it up, it still needs to be here. I think.

…

A mountain still looks like a mountain, doesn't it, after you've drilled out the inside. It doesn't affect the idea of it. No matter what you bury under it, it'll carry on being beautiful. And nobody will notice the difference. As long as we all keep believing in it.

…

Right.

…

I think we all need a drink, eh?

…

I'm buying.

…

Anyone? Mona? Are you going to get behind the bar or would you rather –

…

Do I have to get them myself?

GERRY waits.

Staindrop

A small house in the village of Staindrop, in Teesdale.

AMY's verse in this section is based on the rhythm and rhyme-scheme of the ballad 'Oh!' by John Reed Appleton – published in the Teesdale Mercury on 16th August 1890. The ballad is a satirical imagining of a town preparing to receive a royal visit, which turns out to be a hoax.

In this section MONA MARK and ANDY divide the narrative verse between them.

AMY: In a white house by an old estate

    Home of two women, warm and bounded

    Which although small, supports the weight

    Of dreams and love and plans well-founded

    Where both seem happy with their lot

    And live full lives with schemes they've dreamt

    The house itself part of their plot

    So long as they timely pay the rent

    All the white houses stand on land

    Within the local Baron's orbit

    The castle owns them, takes the rent

    For this and centuries before, it

    Falls to a man to raise the dues

    A local agent of the system

Willing and proud of duty to

Support aristocratic wisdom

In comes a visitor, one they know

Through village life, and tenant's rent

But also through the local flow

The tenuous ties of family bent

To knowledge, everybody knows

The flow of business in a small place

Each knows the others dreams and hopes

Familiar in all as in your own face

Modern the fingers on the keys

To write the stories of our fathers

Ancient the roots of family trees

That lock us in, define our borders

Stay at the level you are put

Closer to surface, ground well trodden

Part of the social fabric, but

Even here, hidden by the modern

On an estate that paints houses white

That's still in thrall to feudal owners

The echoes of the ancient right

To make the poor, half-willing donors

Of time and labour to the cause

Of entrenched privilege's birthright

One branch of blood legitimate

One branch of blood forever twilight

The front room of a house in Staindrop. GERRY has just arrived. AMY is sitting in an armchair. GINNY is standing by the door to the kitchen.

GERRY: Tea.

   …

   Two sugars. Thanks.

GINNY: Milk?

GERRY: If you've got it.

GINNY: We've got –

GERRY: Course you have. I just mean fine if not. If you haven't.

   …

   If you hadn't, I've had had it black.

GINNY: Right.

GERRY: Rather than having something else.

GINNY: Right.

   GINNY leaves. Pause.

AMY: How are things?

GERRY: Which things?

AMY: At the estate?

GERRY: Those things are currently good.

MONA/ MARK/ ANDY: There's a story told round here

    Different versions, depending where you are

    There's the pub story, the castle story

    The street story, the drunk one and the sober

    But if all those versions shared a title

    It would be 'Why The Houses Are White'

    The purpose of every version is the same

    It's explained by the title pretty well

    You'll notice, round here, in the villages

    And on and up the valley past High Force

    Some of the buildings stand exceeding bright

    Jewelled against the green and grey

    Against the landscape, unmissable

    Even in the foulest weather, and it does

    Get pretty foul up here, rain in long shrouds

    Bringing a dullness to the beauty, still

    Beautiful, though, and the snow in winter

    Blown harsh across the eyes to burn them blind

    The buildings glow like pearls thrown in a well

The story tells the origin of that

The opalescence of those whitewashed walls

Explains why they're so bright, and what they mean

AMY: If this is in any way official –

GERRY: How are things with you?

AMY: I'm just saying, if this is business, talk to the wife.

GERRY: Absolutely. But how *are* –

AMY: I'm sorry about the smell.

GERRY: What smell?

AMY: If it smells of dog. Died two weeks ago.

GERRY: I'm sorry.

AMY: Don't be. She was old. But you know what it is. When you live with an animal, you never know if the smell's still there or not when the animal's gone, because you never really noticed it anyway.

   …

So if it is there, I apologise.

GERRY: I can't smell anything.

   …

I can't smell dog. Obviously I can smell a variety of things but they're all pleasant.

AMY: Well that's a relief.

Pause. GINNY comes in with two mugs of tea. She gives one to GERRY and puts the other down beside AMY.

He's here on business.

GINNY: Is he?

GERRY: I didn't say that.

   …

   Tea's nice.

GINNY: Good.

   …

   How's things up at the estate, Gerry?

AMY: He says they're good.

GINNY: Are they?

GERRY: Yeah. Making progress.

MONA/ MARK/ ANDY: Anyway, there was this Lord, a Lord

   Just like there is now, but different

   Because the times were different back then

   It was an age of chivalry, or peasantry

   Or cruelty, or even something golden

   Beyond the pedestrian dreams we wander in

   Of smartphones, instant meals and council tax

   It was the fifteenth century, or maybe

   The seventeenth, or, well it depends

   But, for sure, a time before antibiotics

   When winter firewood was a matter of survival

   And to be anyone, you had to have a horse

   A different bond of service to the land, as well

Vast swathes, even more than now, under

The keen observance of a huge estate

A time of tithes, and the trade

Of wool or crops controlled by levied tax

So not that different in some ways, too

Except the levy far more personal

And the goods more tangible, but there we are

Harsher than now, or at least more naked

The machinations of the state less hidden

The main thing though, is it was winter

All versions of this agree it was winter

Because without that, it simply doesn't work

It was winter, and there was a Lord

And this Lord was, well, he was many Lords

A man for sure, all tales agree on that

But in the castle's version, noble, kind

And in the version told in certain pubs

A bastard of the old school, rude and cruel

In other pubs that use a later date, a dandy, maybe

Laced, dressed, pompadoured like an alien prince

Or just some lucky bastard gained a hold

Because his father's cousin knew a Queen

A gentle man, intelligent and kind

Acute in care for tenant farmers' needs

An ignorant, whip-toting gangster boy

Who never knew the bite of poverty

All these things he is, the Lord, and none

But he existed, that's the point, every tale

Insists on this point clearly, he was real

Not only real, but every tale is true

A fact that happened, to explain the now

Because of course the Lord exists

And the houses he owns, white

GINNY: So is the rent going up?

GERRY: Why would you think that?

GINNY: Why would I not think that?

GERRY: Ma said she saw you up in Cockfield the other day.

GINNY: How old is she now?

GERRY: Eighty-seven, I think, I stopped counting.

AMY: You should probably check that Gerry.

GERRY: Aye.

GINNY: Still got all her faculties though.

GERRY: She's sharper than me.

GINNY: Good eyesight too.

GERRY: What were you doing up there?

GINNY: Just wandering around. Went up the old mine
workings.

GERRY: That's a good walk.

GINNY: Fucked my shoes.

GERRY: Yeah. It's a good walk if you've got the right
footwear.

GINNY: It's amazing how the ground holds the water. Must
have been a nightmare keeping it out of the workings.

GERRY: They were never that deep. Not there.

Pause.

Are you coming to the open day?

AMY: Doubt it.

GERRY: You should.

AMY: Why?

GERRY: You're tenants. It's free.

AMY: Oh. Well in that case –

GERRY: You'll come?

AMY: No.

Pause.

GINNY: Is the rent going up?

GERRY: There's a craft fair.

…

Medieval arts and crafts.

AMY: Witch burning?

GERRY: Don't be daft.

> …

> We mostly hanged them round here.

> *Pause.*

> Falconry.

GINNY: Near a road?

GERRY: Last one was in 1792.

> …

> Road?

GINNY: I saw on YouTube the other day. Outtake from a documentary. There's this guy. Old guy. Properly skilled. They're interviewing him about birds of prey. He's got a falcon looped onto his wrist. Anyway, they talk a bit. I think it's in Wales. Or one of the Baltics. Then he lets it go, and it flies off in this massive arc, like this shallow circle, and the camera follows it. Like this incredibly wide circle centred on the trainer. You can see what a job he's done. Like, he's literally the centre of this bird's world. Then about halfway round the circle it swings across a road, which you haven't seen before cos of the camera angle, and it goes full tilt into the windscreen of a truck coming the other way. Incredibly sudden. And there's a pause, and the trainer says – we lost a good bird today.

> …

> You've not seen it? About three million people have watched that.

GERRY: That sounds horrible.

GINNY: Yeah I'm not saying it's not horrible. I'm just saying I hope you've taken the possibility into account.

Pause.

GERRY: Well there's falconry. And a general, you know, bird of prey display. And a hog roast and a vegetarian hog-roast alternative. His Lordship'll be there, naturally.

…

I just thought it'd be a nice day out for you. Flags on tents. Demonstrations.

GINNY: Against what?

GERRY: Of fighting.

AMY: Great.

…

Well we'll have a think, Gerry. If we fancy a pork sandwich while we're watching two men in tin cans pretend to twat each other, we'll come along.

MONA/ MARK/ ANDY: So, the story, let's have the details

Every single teller can agree on

It is, no matter the year, dead winter

After the feasting, but before the sun finds fire

Snow lies, but not too deep, the ground

Frozen hard, stiff as a family tree

It's surprising the horses' hooves don't spark

So it is cold, fatal cold if anything should pass

To trap unfortunate travellers overnight

The sky at daybreak, let's say it's blue

A gorgeous over-arching vault of boundless depth

Without a breath of wind, or lick of warmth

But bright and crystal clear, the hills

Rising either side of the Tees, channeling

The river in its rock-strewn course, are magic

Receding until lost to sight from distance

But every contour picked out with a sharpness

Echoing the sharpness of his Lordship's mind

He has breakfasted, the great man

Eaten, let's say, dried beef, apples

That sounds about right, dried beef

At breakfast seems appropriately rich

Porridge from a kitchen cauldron

Served by those awake for hours

Provisions robustly stowed in saddlebags

He walks the stables, instructs the grooms

As they prepare his mounts for his domain

Perhaps he chides them, perhaps slaps backs

Depending on whose eyes transmit the tale

AMY: By the way, Gerry. I never got the email with next
month's rota.

GERRY: You didn't?

AMY: Will you send it?

GERRY: Sure thing.

    …

    While I'm here, is there anything needs doing?

GINNY: Like what?

GERRY: Just asking generally. Maintenance.

AMY: You offering to do some DIY?

GERRY: Well I think that's best done by qualified professionals.

AMY: Wouldn't want to risk the market value of the property.

GERRY: More like we want to look after our tenants.

GINNY: You could clear the bodies out of the cellar.

GERRY: What?

GINNY: I said there's a washer going on one of the bath taps.

GERRY: I'll get that seen to.

    Pause.

GINNY: So the fair, Gerry. Will there be some sort of celebrity guest?

GERRY: Apart from his Lordship?

GINNY: No, I meant an actual celebrity.

    Pause.

GERRY: Some fella from Bishop FM, if that counts.

    Pause.

GERRY: So. The rent *is* going up –

GINNY: Bam. And the falcon goes right in the fucking windscreen.

GERRY: It's not like it hasn't happened before.

GINNY: Do you want us out?

GERRY: It's not a lot. Percentage-wise.

   …

   Of course we don't want you out.

GINNY: What's all the 'we' stuff? I said – do *you* want us out?

GERRY: Why would I –

   …

   No. Of course not.

AMY: But it's just us?

GERRY: No. I mean everyone's rent's going up. To some degree.

   …

   Across the board.

GINNY: So you're visiting everyone are you? Every tenant? Personally?

GERRY: No. That'd be massively impractical.

AMY: Well. Aren't we lucky?

GINNY: Not everyone gets a personal visit from the landlord's agent. Not these days.

AMY: I guess that's the way it's always been.

…

You're a fine man, Gerry. Carrying the burden of tradition
so well.

MONA/ MARK/ ANDY: The Lord is great, no question, in his way

How else could he have so many at command

No other explanation bears much weight

It can't be simple luck, must be a quality

That fosters our belief and holds him here

The horse's breath condenses, ice in air

Her flanks are warm under his noble hand

If this was a film, the way he touched his horse

Would tell us in an second how to feel

He stands beside the walls, looks down Low Pond

The rank of trees with darkness wisped beneath

He feels the weight of his riding cloak

The supple leather of his hand sewn gloves

He feels the burn of his anticipation

The sweet draught of air in a free man's lungs

Gathers his party, no other nobles with him

Two horses, two dogs, a groom, a pack-man

Ready to gut and dress what deer the dogs might down

Closes his eyes, holds that scene in his head
The long castle wall, the still water, edge of trees
Cannot imagine it would ever change
As stable as the power he sits upon
As perfect edge to edge as winter sky

And then rides out, crossbow at the ready
Or hunting gun, depending on the tale
Crosses the boundary of the castle
The dogs in full-throated chase, and leaps
Across a stream, the field behind the church
Then wheels the mount to face the open moors
The miles from here to upland eaten up
In rushing wind that scours the noble cheek
Leans forward in the saddle, shouts them on
Skirts rocks, jumps walls, scatters knots of sheep
Each hoofbeat on a patch of earth he owns
Feeling the energy of England in each stride
The mythic real, the history as fire
Cold, golden, molten in the veins of land
Each beat, a chorus drum that builds to him
An owner, steward now of royal flame
Or his part of it, not to be a King

But faithful stone in wall supporting one

With all the benefit that duty brings

Including this, to ride your land, kill your deer

Scramble over your own rocks on your own hills

Feel nothing but your mastery of all

GERRY: I just don't want you to think, given –

AMY: Here we go –

GERRY: Given your history of –

…

I just don't want you to take it personally. I know things are, fraught at the moment, and I wouldn't want you to think this was in any way personal.

AMY: Do I look like I'm flying off the handle, Gerry?

GERRY: I slightly resent the suggestion that I'm the unreasonable one here.

GINNY: Nobody's being unreasonable.

Pause.

Although in the interest of full disclosure, Gerry. And I'm sorry about this, for the record. When I was in the kitchen I wiped one of my fingers right round my arsehole and I stuck it in your tea.

Pause. GERRY raises his tea. Looks at GINNY. Very slowly and deliberately takes a sip, takes a letter out of his pocket.

GERRY: Right. Well I wanted to hand-deliver this. Like I said, everyone else is getting theirs in the post, but I didn't want you to misread it as specifically targeted at you.

GINNY: Why would we do that?

Pause.

GERRY: I just don't want anyone to get the wrong idea.

AMY: About what?

…

Hey. Why don't you tell Gerry about your project? The one for your dissertation.

GINNY: Really?

AMY: Go on. I think he'll be interested.

…

Right up your street, that, Gerry. Genealogy. GERRY: Can you even do a degree in that?

GINNY: It's not in that. It's a just project on research practice. I had to choose something to research, so I thought I'd do the family.

GERRY: Good on you. Going back into education at your age.

GINNY: I'm twenty-nine.

…

Anyway. It's not that interesting. Just decided to do some family research.

GERRY: I started a bit of that once.

…

Not family, as such. Just started to look back into old records at the castle.

…

The bloody handwriting alone. I sometimes think they did it on purpose. Of course they didn't. In fact it's us who's lost a skill. That's what makes it so hard to read. And of course the age of the documents. And the fact that they weren't as profligate with resources as us, were they?

…

Used every spare space on the paper. I think I showed you.

AMY: I remember. It's an odd thing to look at. These people, a lot of them. Vital to keep a system working, but still basically disposable. Interchangeable. All recorded. All entered in the ledger.

…

Like keeping livestock. Like tagging deer.

MONA/ MARK/ ANDY: It is a stag of course, the first they find

How could it not be on a glorious day

Dogs catching scent first, then rushing in

As it bolts redly from a stand of trees

And pours like spirit up a sheep-cleared slope

On, through tied farms, up the valley side

On, the dogs ahead all flecks of spit

On into trackless moorland, where the mind

Flies skyward with the vast expanse of it

The stag's hooves clattering madly in a gully

The dogs turn quickly, groom and pack-man follow

The Lord behind, driving his mount until

He pulls up sharply in a slate-grey hollow

He is alone

The Lord looks skyward, feels one breath of wind

A single movement of the air for now, he strains

To hear the bark of dog or slip of hoof

But in the gully silence tyrant reigns

AMY: Do you know what a consanguinity index is, Gerry?

GERRY: I've heard of it.

AMY: I hadn't. Until she started going on about it the other night.

…

Go on. Tell him.

GINNY: I'll leave it, thanks.

GERRY: No, go on.

GINNY: Basically it allows the assignation of a numerical value between zero and one to the level of blood relation between two people. So me and my identical twin, if I had one, we're essentially clones. Genetically identical. So that value would be one. Me and someone completely unrelated, zero.

…

As close to zero as makes no difference. I mean, not that any of us are completely unrelated. Shared ancestry if you go back far enough down any line. We're all related to Charlemagne. Or, everyone's from Africa originally. All that.

…

It's all pretty easy to understand, mathematically. So you and your siblings have an index of point five with your parents. Assuming your parents weren't related in any significant way. That pushes it higher than point five. The higher it's pushed, the more closely related your parents.

…

So, you know, if you're tracing family trees, a score for how inbred you are. They use it a lot in articles about the peerage. You know. Massive, interrelated families that quite often have a reason not to marry outside of a defined pool of potential mates. Works for everyone else too, though. I suppose it is fascinating. Genealogically speaking.

Pause.

Dave from the pub said you were putting a new bathroom in.

GERRY: I'm sorry?

GINNY: At your mum's place. He said you were putting a new bathroom in. You'd asked him about it, anyway. What does she need a new bathroom for at eighty-seven?

…

Or whatever age she is?

GERRY: Yeah, I might have mentioned. No concrete plans though. It was more a theoretical conversation.

Pause.

GINNY: Still. When she does die, you'll get the house, so I suppose you want to think about tiling and stuff. Taps.

GERRY: Oh, I imagine she's got years in her yet.

MONA/ MARK/ ANDY: Now, here's where all the tales agree

The ones where he is kind and the ones

Where he's less kind, the weather closes in

The weather can do that round here

It can do it in an instant, this place

Is small enough to have its own relationship, still

With weather, so the Lord climbs from the gully

Skitters his horse onto the moorland, expecting

To see his dogs, his men, maybe receding

Against the blue sky, dots even on the horizon

But actually to see them, follow, catch them

He emerges on the moor top, and is blind

The blue vault has slammed shut its doors

Arches heavy as some future alloy

Seemingly without a wind to drive them

The clouds, cold-moisture-pregnant

Have swept up from the sea, against hill air

And found a stillness just above the moor

A single flake of snow settles on the horse's brow

And lies there, winning battle with the creature's heat

And then another. And another.

And then a full force blizzard, closing down the world.

GERRY: Oh. Almost forgot.

GERRY rummages in his bag. Takes out a small tin of shortbread biscuits.

Are these yours?

AMY takes the biscuits and examines them. Stares at GERRY.

We had a clear out of the cupboards in the break room. Nobody claimed these. Someone thought they might be yours. Didn't want to waste them.

AMY opens the biscuits.

I checked. They're still good.

AMY: Wow. That's –

…

That's thoughtful, Gerry.

GERRY: It's no problem.

AMY: I mean you could have just waited til I got back to work. But you didn't.

…

Ginny, shall we celebrate?

GINNY: Celebrate?

AMY: The miraculous return of my biscuits. I mean, an event like this requires something stronger than tea, wouldn't you agree?

GINNY: What are you thinking?

AMY: Well I know it's a little early, but perhaps you could go into the kitchen and fetch three glasses and a bottle of the good rum.

GERRY: Well. I'm driving, so –

AMY: Come on Gerry. You can have one.

…

Ginny?

GINNY: Well absolutely.

AMY: And Ginny, fetch the good glasses please. The tumblers. The ones with the heavy bottoms.

GINNY: I'll just be a sec.

GINNY goes into the kitchen.

AMY: This is lovely, Gerry. Thank you.

GERRY: There's no need to make a fuss.

AMY: How is everything, by the way? At the gift shop?

GERRY: Oh it's ticking over.

AMY: Good to hear.

GERRY: We've started a new line.

AMY: That's nice.

GERRY: Replica halberds. Tiny ones. They work as letter-openers.

Pause.

AMY: Good. Well I'll look forward to getting to grips with those on Monday.

Pause.

The guy was a fucking racist, Gerry.

GERRY: He was a member of a coach party.

AMY: He had a Confederate Flag on his backpack.

GERRY: That doesn't necessarily mean –

AMY: He was pontificating, Gerry. He was using the fact Jeremiah Dixon grew up down the road from here to insinuate some kind of connection with the South in the Civil War. Jeremiah Dixon drew the battle line, he said, and the wrong side won.

…

It's not even like Jeremiah Dixon knew what the Mason Dixon line was going to mean. He was just some guy from Cockfield that got sent to America to survey a border. You can't pin any of that on him.

…

All I did was make my feelings clear.

GERRY: "Get the fuck out of my gift shop you redneck prick."

…

No. I'm not re-litigating this. It is not up for re-litigation.

AMY: Re-litigation?

…

When did you start talking like Kellyanne fucking Conway?

GINNY comes back with a tray, a bottle of rum, three heavy glass tumblers, rum in the glasses.

GINNY/ MONA/ MARK: Let's have a drink, eh?

> Hours it seems he wheels the horse about
>
> Searching for some landmark on the trackless moor

ANDY: Blind by the cold fragments of dead stars

> The only sound the horse's breath and his
>
> The jingle of harness, as even the falling hoof
>
> Fades on a thickening sheet of white
>
> He sets out one way, feels the land rise, turns
>
> Sets out another, the ground begins to fall
>
> So inch by perilous inch he has to crawl
>
> Avoid the deadly heights as much as deadly drop
>
> And even through his cloak the needles run
>
> His gloves the best the makers could produce
>
> Let in frost's skinny fingers, clamped across his own
>
> Even the horse, best beast in a harsh county
>
> Begins to lose one trembling step in ten
>
> And then in five, his mind fills with a dream
>
> Of flint and tinder in the pack-man's pack
>
> That might be on the moon for all its use
>
> And still snow falls, not once a curtain twitch
>
> That lets him see a foot past his own hands

GINNY: Here's to. Here's to what?

AMY: The return of the prodigal biscuits.

GINNY: Fair enough.

They all drink.

GERRY: Well. Before I head off.

…

There was something I wanted to give you a bit of a heads-up about. Since you've brought it up.

MONA/ MARK/ ANDY: For hours it seems he skirts the sight of death

The day draws darker, snow surrounds them still

They feel their faltering way, outflank this hill

Follow that stream, familiar or not

His wandering mind cannot impose his land

His knowledge of his property, on this alien world

And grey creeps out of ground and air alike

Then black, it swallows them, and now he thinks

Of what his tomb might look like

Maybe two stone dogs

Flanking his chest, arms crossed

Not a shield, too ancient, but perhaps

A reference in a stone-laboured epitaph

To this heroic hunt in Staindrop Church

Except it's not heroic, as death comes ever close

He cannot see the link between

Its poetry and him, he is, he knows

A small man on a larger animal

Spilling his last clutched warmth

Across an earth he's fooled himself

And others that he owns, but now he understands

Cares not at all for him, has never known

His ownership or even registered

Him, his mind wanders, not even

Cold now, horse stumbles barely

Breathing, sinks to its

Knees in drifts, oblivion

Leaping at

Them both

And then, a light

GERRY: Amy.

    …

    Look.

    Pause.

AMY: Spit it out, Gerry.

GERRY: There's been a development.

AMY: What?

GERRY: The situation at work. There was something I wanted to speak to you about –

GINNY: Oh, by the way Gerry. I just had a thought. While I was in the kitchen.

GINNY pours herself another rum.

It set me thinking. Here I am, doing this project on the roots of my family. And here you are, what are we? Second cousins once removed I thought, but apparently, it's third cousins. You're the child of my dad's second cousin, which means, essentially, we share a great grandparent. But who round here doesn't?

…

We don't have a very high consanguinity index, by the way Gerry, unless something's gone slightly awry with the old inbreeding. It's not like we own a castle though, so it's unlikely.

GERRY: Well that's a relief.

GINNY: Isn't it?

MONA/ MARK/ ANDY: Some fever dream or not he cannot tell

But just one crack, the drifting wall of flakes

Lets in a spark that lasts, fixed, wavering

But real, a fire that leaps in some true grate

The Lord spurs the horse, the last strength

Wavering in both man and animal

Across the valley floor, plunges and flounders

Through a leaping stream, ice-edged

Up to a cottage door, a labourer he thinks

One of the other animals that make their sweat

His gold, cowering here against the storm

Not nobly battling the elements, but warm

A lifeline for a Lord in desperate straits

He ties the horse in shelter by the eaves

Stagger his last steps through thigh-deep drifts

Beats at the door with palms both numb and raw

Fights the urge to kneel, stays dignified

AMY: Anyone?

GINNY: Aye.

AMY pours GINNY some rum.

AMY: Gerry?

GERRY: No. Thanks.

AMY: We should get another dog.

…

Don't mind me. I was drinking well before you got here.

Pause.

GERRY: Look. While I'm here. I need to talk to you about
Monday.

AMY: What about it?

GERRY: I think there's a –

…

There's a general consensus. That you should possibly take a little more time off.

AMY: How much time off?

GERRY: We don't know yet.

Pause.

I didn't. I wasn't sure I should say anything, but I didn't want you hearing about it from anyone else.

AMY: You're suspending me.

GERRY: I wouldn't call it that. The feeling is we need a little more time to think about what to do, going forward.

Pause.

There'll be a letter, Obviously. And it doesn't mean, by any means that you'll. That this is a hard and fast decision. You'll get your opportunity to respond. I just. The general feeling is people need more time to think about –

Pause.

AMY: So this is it, really, isn't it?

…

Will we have to move out?

GERRY: Jesus, of course you won't have to move out.

…

Since when do you have to be an estate employee to rent a house?

AMY: I thought I was just being suspended?

GERRY: It's not a foregone conclusion.

77

AMY: Fucking hell, Gerry, I actually liked that job.

GERRY: I know.

   …

   But there's the fallout to consider.

AMY: I don't remember seeing it in the Mercury.

GERRY: Well you wouldn't, would you?

   …

   It's not the local press. It's just a fact. Given the way things might go. Economically. Nobody knows, do they. How important visitors like that –

AMY: Americans?

GERRY: Not just Americans. As such. We're heading into uncertain times and we can't afford to be alienating potential sources of revenue.

AMY: So people are just allowed to say what they want now, because we're too scared of the money going away.

GERRY: Its just. It's not a good look, Amy.

   …

   It's a precarious situation.

AMY: Really? Hundreds of years of this, and suddenly it's a precarious situation?

GERRY: You can't come back on Monday.

   Pause.

   That's the upshot of it. That's the headline. So don't.

   …

Please.

Pause.

GINNY: Before you go, Gerry.

…

I never finished telling you about the college course.

…

So I'm doing this project. Here, living in this house, renting it from a feudal estate, looking into my own family tree, which is kind of yours too obviously. Thinking about how this stuff isn't really at your fingertips, if you're not from a family worth writing down. Thinking about heritage. How it expresses itself differently according to class background.

…

Do you want to know something, Gerry?

GERRY starts to get up.

I think it's nice, by the way. Only child. Never married. Looked after his mum. You get the house, don't you?

GERRY: Who else?

GINNY: Well, nobody. That's the point. We get what we deserve. Here you are, managing the rentals for all the houses the Estate owns, and you don't even have a house of your own. But obviously you will have. At some point.

GERRY: I'm in no rush.

GINNY: Well, obviously.

…

Nothing to worry about.

…

You've always had family working for the Estate, haven't
you? Going way back.

MONA/ MARK/ ANDY: The door opens, and there stands a man

The product of a life upon this hill

Shifting stones, clearing streams, hewing

Wood, keeping animals in bounds

The man eyes the Lord, Lord eyes the man

A silence as the warmth seeps round him from

The fire-lit room beyond, two chairs

Dirt floor, stone walls, a woman mends a shirt

The Lord steps in

And now the tales depart on their own paths

Although in every version the Lord needs help

In some he demands, threatens, simply

Walks in, takes food, shelter, warmth

In others he is polite, asks sanctuary

Throws himself on hospitality, seeks

Human to human to wait out the storm

It all depends, the where of telling it

Front room, cafe, castle, late-night pub

Whether we're drinking hard or sipping tea

Or who heard this from whom and when they did

The closeness of the teller to their facts

Tenant, poacher, gamekeeper, someone

Who rails against immigrants tells a different tale

From someone who came here a year ago

The heritage-maintainers have their line

The modern-thinking democrats, theirs too

The labour voters' story differs hard

From those whose politics shade darker blue

They'll tell you endings that support their ends

GERRY: Of course. Uncle was a gamekeeper.

AMY: I remember you told me that.

…

You seemed very proud of that.

GERRY: I am.

…

He used to take me up there when I was a kid. Look at the deer.

…

They can be invisible if they want to be. That was what he used to say.

GERRY pours himself another rum.

Any weather. Fog, obviously, but rain, snow, summer sun. They've got a way of making themselves invisible if they don't want to be seen.

…

Not true of course. Not literally. But I thought it was magic.

…

Never thought I'd be working there. Thought it was fairyland.

GINNY: It is a magic, kind of, Gerry. The whole thing's a spell. They don't really have what we have round here anywhere else.

…

Not any more. I mean it all used to be like this. But round here there's a relic of something still living that's mostly died off in other places.

Pause.

Anyway. Here am I. All high and mighty. Getting on my high horse about the fact that so much of the life around here seems to have been dedicated to supporting and maintaining a system that doesn't necessarily work in the interests of the people.

…

And of course we still live in that relic. Literally in our case.

GERRY: It's not a relic though, is it?

…

Look at the employment it provides.

AMY: Not for long in my case.

GERRY: It's a suspension.

AMY: Until it's a sacking.

GINNY: Here I am, though. Knowing what side I'm on in the debate.

...

Of course I share blood with people on the other side. Not the people at the top, obviously. People like you, who've been instrumental in keeping the whole thing ticking over for so long.

...

But I don't share that much blood, do I? And anyway, even if we are related, we're both on the same side of the fence. We're both on the outside, looking in.

...

And then guess what I found?

GERRY: What?

GINNY: I found this woman. Her name was Ann Charlton.

GERRY: Charlton.

GINNY: Hasn't been a name in the family for years, has it?

GERRY: I don't even recall.

GINNY: Was probably the last surname our families shared. Common ancestor, kind of thing.

GERRY: When was this?

GINNY: Eighteen seventy or thereabouts.

...

So that'd make her my great-great-great grandmother.

GERRY: Would it?

GINNY: And your great-great grandmother. Last direct relative we have in common.

...

Listed occupation at the time she gave birth, domestic help.

AMY: Married?

GINNY: Course she wasn't married.

...

Anyway. Ann Charlton was domestic help. Up at the castle. Of course they had to let her go. Got pregnant, didn't she.

...

History doesn't relate who the father was. Could have been anyone I suppose.

AMY: Lucky she wasn't sent to America.

...

Or unlucky.

...

You could be American, Gerry. Think of that. Or bits of you could. Coming back here to visit the old country. Could have been you in the bloody gift shop.

...

Still. We're all just DNA aren't we, really. Passing itself on in ways that get recognised or not recognised.

MONA/ MARK/ ANDY: The different versions of the tale diverge

The Lord is welcomed, given food and warmth

Stays the night with his tenant friends

Humbly amazed to host their master there

And in the morning sallies out across clear air

Across deep snow, and leaving deeper thanks

Or, hospitality is still willingly given

As he'd presumed it would be, spends

A night by the fire and not til morning light

Discovers from the man or woman

Their humble house owes nothing to his might

And his presumption falters, shamed he has assumed

Their tenancy, and by doing so

Lorded himself so naturally over two

Who took him in without one question or complaint

Or in the darker version of the tale

Darker, but never told without a glint of pleasure

The Lord, his arrogance, entitled even now

At risk of death, demands his right

Demanding recognition he steps in

Only to have the farmer bar his way

Talks to him like some medieval serf

Explains in brutish terms his ownership

Not just of the house itself, the land its on

The very stones that bond to make its walls

Not just their food and drink, the folk themselves

In this tale now the Lord is raving mad

From the perspective of the farmer and his wife

Who live outside the bounds of his estate

Have paid him not one penny their whole life

The farmer turns him out into the snow

Seeing his arrogance as danger, and

The Lord, weakened and still lost goes out

And dies, ice-solid in the iron night

GERRY: What did she do after that?

GINNY: Stayed around here. Died in Durham. No occupation listed.

GERRY: How old?

GINNY: Thirty-seven.

GERRY: When she had the baby?

GINNY: Oh. Seventeen.

...

She was probably a maid. They weren't very specific about occupations. I mean domestic help was domestic help.

...

I doubt your job title's much more than that, is it?

…

But I got curious. Looked her up. One report in the local paper. Not long after she gave birth. Turned up drunk at the castle gates and had to be detained. Madwoman, they thought she was. Waving a baby around and screaming about wanting to show him his birthright.

…

Gave the baby into the care of his grandmother and kind of disappeared until she dies in Durham aged thirty-seven.

Pause.

I mean none of it proves anything. Interesting thought, though, that the difference between us on one side of the wall and the ones on the other is just who gets legitimately fucked.

GERRY: You have absolutely no fucking idea what it takes to hold a community together. There are some things at the edges, and you have to decide they don't matter for the centre to hold. And it's easy to decide they don't matter. Because they don't.

…

So. Here's the official notice of the rent increase. I'll post the official notice of the suspension as soon as I'm back in the office.

GERRY puts the envelope down.

I'd better get back to it.

…

The open day's not going to arrange itself.

MONA/ MARK/ ANDY: Whatever the details of each tale

The result, the thing done, is the same

Either, in the tales the Lord survives, by him

Or by his heirs in the more vengeful ones

The freezing to death ones

The should have treated us better ones

The why is this still happening ones

To avoid confusion in noble minds

Or embarrassment perhaps in future blizzards,

Or any other time a Lord might need

To assert his dominance, control over his property

He decrees, or his heirs decree the same

That every house he owns, no others

Should be white-painted, visible, both from a distance

And as a mark of ownership, unmistakable

AMY: Hope it doesn't end up feeling like Bullseye. Going into work.

GERRY: Bullseye?

AMY: Surely you remember Bullseye?

   …

If they fucked up the last dart. You know. Missed out on the star prize?

   …

They used to pull the screen back and show them anyway, didn't they? 'Here's what you could have won', and fucking hell it's a speedboat or whatever. Not that a castle was ever a prize on Bullseye.

…

Here's what you could have won.

GERRY: Why would I think of it like that?

AMY: Well. Now you can. You're welcome.

Pause.

GERRY: It won't feel like that at all.

GINNY: Well. Good for you.

GERRY: There's a particular view. Not really a time of year for it. It can just catch you. I've never been able to work out if it's the mood you're in, or something particular about the weather. Time of day. Maybe the light.

…

I'm standing where the path crosses the land between High Pond and Low Pond. And I look across the length of Low Pond towards the Castle.

…

Right up the length of the water, up to that great flat wall at the end of it, with everything else just piled on top.

…

I'll tell you what it is. It's a day when there's nothing in the way. No distractions. No tents up in the grounds or parked cars. Maybe a couple of deer in the distance. And it's not about the sun. It's the wind. Or lack of it. No ripples on the water.

…

Like that painting. Alexander Frances Lydon. We sell them in the gift shop. Remember?

AMY: I remember.

GERRY: And I think, I'm a part of this. Somewhere in me. I'm helping this continue. And I'll be gone one day. And that'd be true whether I was in a bedroom up the tower or standing here. But this will still be here, and one of the reasons it'll still be here will be me. And it's good. That it's here. Despite what people might or might not have done to each other. Despite what it might mean to some people, and the different things it means to others. And I'm alright with that. That's what I feel. Not happy, or sad, just. Alright with it.

GINNY: Is that enough?

GERRY: Yes, it's enough.

GINNY: Really?

GERRY: What's the point, really, of being angry with history?

GINNY: What's the point of not? All the white houses are still owned.

GERRY: All houses are owned by someone.

…

You make your living off this just as much as I do.

AMY: Made.

GERRY: Well maybe it's time for a change.

…

I mean you complain, but you're still here. Plenty of places to go where they do things differently.

GINNY: So you want us out?

GERRY: Christ, of course I don't.

    …

    I'm just saying maybe you should think about what your options are.

    …

    Maybe I should too.

GINNY: But you won't, will you?

GERRY: Probably not.

AMY: You know what I'd love to think, Gerry? That one day you'll look at all the things you just described. The old walls, and the light on the lake, and the rutting stags or whatever. And just for a second, you'll want to set it all on fire.

GERRY: Who says I don't think that, sometimes?

GINNY: So why don't you?

GERRY: Because some things are bigger than the people in them.

MONA/ MARK/ ANDY: So that is why, driving here now

    No fear of weather, heaters on

    Or else walking the moor, seeing a blizzard

    In your phone's weather app, or

    Tracking your way with loss-preventing GPS

    You will see every tale's result

    Scattered solid across the landscape

    From castle to village to valley's head

Nestled in forest or proudly on farm track

Cheek by jowl with crossroad pub

Or glinting in the middle of a terrace

Those white houses, painted by decree

And still symbolic of an ownership

That runs through and over all this land

Like coal through seams, history in blood trees

An England under England

That has not faded yet.

Whitby

The headland near the Royal Hotel, Whitby. MARK stands, looking down over the harbour.

NB – MARK's verses in this scene are to the rhythm and rhyme scheme of 'Heartland' by The Sisters of Mercy.

MARK: Lay me down upon the quay

Upon the swallowed bones of sea, the

Lashing storms of ages past

Buoy up my heart, entomb me fast

Lay me down upon the quay

The crushing weight of history, the

Vampires, trawlers, priests and miners

All that ties this place to me

Last of sunset light now falls

On silhouetted Abbey walls

The harbour gathers in the dark

As moorland fades and future calls

GINNY: Let me tell you. Poor men doing a rich man's work for him. And the rich man praying for a storm to lose the boat. Because they weren't more than pack animals, were they? Animals to move his money around. And animals aren't worth the feeding and the care if they're not bringing a return. You might as well cut your losses and send them to the slaughter. Meat for the fishes. Then maybe there'll be more fish. That's how it used to be.

GERRY and MONA in the office at the arcade. The space is cramped. A small desk. Papers and files. A walkie-talkie. A couple of CCTV monitors. Two chairs. GERRY sits at the desk, MONA stands.

GERRY: You came.

MONA: Said I would.

Pause.

GERRY: What did you tell the choir? Practice tonight, isn't it?

MONA: Jesus, Gerry, this isn't a fucking spy novel.

…

I don't have to tell anyone where I'm going.

Pause.

I know it's been a while. I'm sorry.

GERRY: I understand.

…

How many different ways can I say it's alright for you to come here?

…

It's been a year.

MONA: Christ. Where does it go.

GERRY: Flown by, hasn't it?

Pause.

How's things at the fishing school?

MONA: Got some good ones at the moment. Talented. All there for the right reasons.

GERRY: Great.

MONA: I mean. There's nobody.

…

There's nobody exceptional. But they're good kids. Quick on the uptake.

Turn their hands to anything.

GERRY: Any for the trawlers?

MONA: One. Maybe two. We'll have to see how things change, won't we?

GERRY: Do you think they're likely to?

MONA: To be honest.

…

I have no idea if this is for better or worse. I don't think anyone has. But there'll still be boats, won't there. Boats and ships. So.

Pause.

And yourself?

GERRY: Lights are still flashing. People still like flashing lights. That'll never change. An arcade looks after itself. Good job too. Some days I wonder why I'm here at all.

MONA: Thought you might go into politics.

GERRY: Fuck that.

MONA: You'd be good at it.

GERRY: I'm doing good here.

…

People think this is about taking the money and fuck everyone else. It's not. Do you know how many meetings I've been to with the council?

MONA: About what?

GERRY: You name it. Parking. Street lights. Fucking Christmas lights. Not living in the fucking past. I can't be doing with it. I've given up.

…

Three grand. I offered them. Three and a half. Said I'd do the whole street to start them off. Make it look like Blackpool. Better than that because it wouldn't be shit.

…

Stop living in the past, I said. By all means bring them in for the Dracula Tours. Because that's how we'll survive. But the things that have gone from here aren't necessarily coming back. We live more off the memory we used to fish than fishing. And that's fine. It's what we are now.

…

Course they can just blame it on Scarborough can't they. We'd love to, but this isn't where the decisions get made.

MONA: What am I doing, then? There've been times it's felt like I've been keeping something alive that shouldn't be.

GERRY: This is what I mean. What you're doing, it's the right way to go about it. Take the skills and the history and make it work in the world it's actually in. Or the world it might be.

MONA: Knife edge. Golden age or end of the world. Take your pick.

GERRY: Probability. I make my living off it. And I haven't got a fucking clue which way to go on that one.

AMY is outside the Tourist Information Office by the harbour.

AMY: They sing here, they always did

Not the romantic siren sea voices

Although of course the sea is in the songs

And there are shanties

Oh there are so many fucking sea shanties

You could weave a rope with them and hang yourself

So many songs for storms and sandbanks

And the dangers of the deep

Women and children knotting nets

Sending them in long lines down steep streets

To be taken out again in battle

By men who dreamed of them on shore

And oh, the laments, salted sprays of tears

For the bones lost forever, the

Unmarked graves between here and Denmark

Nails working loose from planks

Skeletons swallowed by sand

Skulls home to eels and weed

And the living laments too, to

Love gone cold on shore, and the

Long wind-blown hair of lasses

Or the bonnie shanks of a lad

Gone so far beyond the horizon

With only a sextant for safety

And now –

AMY checks her phone.

Come on. Prick.

ANDY arrives.

You said half-past.

ANDY: I did.

AMY: You're late.

ANDY: I am.

Pause.

So. I've been thinking. Have we got this the right way round? What are we really trying to save here?

AMY: It's not me, is it? It's mainly you. You're trying to save the Tourist Information Office, Andy.

ANDY: Yes. But. What does that *mean*?

AMY: For fuck's sake.

ANDY: What does it *represent*?

AMY: It represents a physical place where tourists can go for information, rather than another restaurant dispensing artfully re-imagined fish & chips.

ANDY: Yes.

AMY: And you would rather it remained a Tourist Information Office.

ANDY: Yes. So.

…

How about this.

…

We can't stop progress. We can only adapt to it. But. Bear with me. Part of that adaptation is to recognise the past, the way things used to be done, as a foundational part of what we are now. You with me?

AMY: No.

ANDY: Good. So the argument is, we don't need a Tourist Information Office because that's not how people get their tourism information any more. And it's a good argument. I mean who reads leaflets these days? Who'd need directions to anywhere?

AMY: That fundamentally ignores –

ANDY: I know it does. I *know*. But for the majority of people it's true. But that's the virtue. We don't do that any more. It's how we *used* to do it. But we don't do it any more.

AMY: Andy. This is –

ANDY: So what does the Tourist Information Office represent? *The way we used to do things.* And the way we used to do things is worth preserving. Especially here. And if the

Tourist Information Office represents the old way we used to carry out one of our biggest industries, tourism, then by definition it's worth preserving as part of our industrial heritage. It isn't about providing tourist information anymore, it's a place that tourists should be able to come to to experience *the way we used to provide tourist information.*

Pause.

AMY: Andy. Why are we here?

ANDY: I need your help.

AMY: To do what?

ANDY: You used to work here.

AMY: Well I don't. Not anymore.

ANDY: They're coming tomorrow. They're starting work.

AMY: So what?

ANDY: So are you not upset that part of our heritage is passing away?

AMY: Jesus wept, Andy. Do you want to get some fucking chips?

MARK on the headland above town.

MARK: Enough live here and feel it's home

This edgeland town that stands alone, as

I grew up it spoke to me

In tongues edged with the call of sea

Enough live here and feel it's home

The world dissolved in rock and foam, the

Moors behind and sea ahead

Are walls around and sky our dome

It wasn't anybody's fault

My gaze turned inward, and I felt

The flashing lights slow to a halt

My bonds of family fade and melt

MONA: I appreciate this, you know, Gerry. Your support.

GERRY: It's a pleasure.

MONA: Not really a pleasure, though, is it?

GERRY takes a roll of banknotes from his pocket. He puts them down on the table.

GERRY: Take what you need.

MONA: What for?

GERRY: I don't know. Where are the kids from?

MONA: All over. Got a couple from Poland. One came from the Philippines. Middlesborough. One or two local.

GERRY: Expensive, coming here.

…

Just thought, if one of them needed anything. Rent or. I dunno. A coat.

MONA: They don't need anything.

…

But it's appreciated.

GERRY: Don't. You'll make me fucking cry.

ANDY and AMY. They are out on the harbour wall, eating chips.

ANDY: It's a trick, my dad used to say. Knowing where to land fish.

...

Used to be, anyway. You'd have to have a keen appreciation for the tiny clues that are expressions of the underlying workings of supply and demand. There's many a skipper broken his foot kicking in the shutters at the fish quay because he got the right catch in at the wrong time or landed the right time at the wrong place.

AMY: I've been thinking.

ANDY: Timing, you see/

AMY: Andy

ANDY: Is everything.

...

Isn't it?

AMY: If you had to tell someone what this place was like.

...

If you walked into a room and there was a bunch of people, say.

ANDY: Well there isn't that.

AMY: But if you had to. It'd be like trying to sing two songs at once.

...

Trying to find new ways to do the old things. Trying to sit on all this history and work out how the world's changing so fast at the same time. Trying to be part of the world while you're still cut off from it. Invite people in to look while keeping the day to day intact.

…

More than two songs.

ANDY: You should go to the folk night. Try and do that. They'd throw you out of the pub.

GERRY and MONA in the arcade office.

MONA: I'm sorry I've not been round.

GERRY: I've been OK. Mona. I've been too busy not to be OK.

MONA: Ginny?

GERRY: Not so busy. Not so OK.

MONA: I was thinking I haven't seen her for a while.

GERRY: Well you wouldn't have, unless you'd been in our front room, because that's pretty much where she's been unless she's in the loo or making a drink.

MONA: I should come.

GERRY: Maybe you should, but you won't, and it's probably for the best.

…

She won't see you. You'll tell her things she doesn't want to hear yet.

MONA: Like what?

GERRY: Same things I tell her. Like she needs to get on with
    her fucking life. You'll be nicer of course. I know she's my
    daughter but even I'm losing patience.

    …

    I'm sick of her, if I'm honest.

MONA: Don't say that.

GERRY: I don't mean it. I don't mean sick of her. Just. Every
    day she gets up and the wind turbines have been in her
    head. In her dreams. That bollocks. As if it's them and not
    the water that killed him.

    …

    He could have jumped in the harbour pissed and drowned
    as easy as jumping –

    Pause.

    You want to go somewhere?

MONA: Like where?

GERRY: Get a drink.

MONA: It's one thing coming here. It's another –

GERRY: I don't give a fuck, to be honest.

MONA: I do.

    …

    People talk.

GERRY: Yeah. Well. If they know what's good for them, they
    don't.

MONA: We're not going back there.

    …

We need to draw a line under this, because it's doing neither of us any good.

GERRY: What are you worried about? We're both –

MONA: I'm not worried what people think, Gerry.

…

I don't regret it happening. But it happened in the first place because we were both so fucking sad.

GERRY: We both seem to –

MONA: Not that. I don't mean the physical stuff.

GERRY: I could have blamed you.

MONA: You'd have been fucking wrong if you did.

GERRY: It wasn't anyone's fault but his.

MONA: It wasn't his fault either.

GERRY: What happened between us after he died. It wasn't me trying to reassure you of anything.

MONA: And it wasn't me thinking I owed you anything.

…

Maybe it stopped us being sad. Or at least sad for the wrong reasons. But don't think for a second I was looking for your forgiveness.

GERRY: I'm not really inclined to analyse it that much.

…

Don't remember either of us being sad when we're up against the desk there.

Pause.

MONA: You're a dinosaur. You know that?

GERRY: If the dinosaurs were anything like me, the fuckers would still be alive.

MONA: Course they would.

Noise of shouting from the arcade. MONA reacts. GERRY doesn't.

GERRY: It's alright.

MONA: Doesn't sound like it.

GERRY: You haven't got your ear in is all.

…

So many years I've been listening to bother through that wall, I can tell what's going to be serious and what's not in about half a second. Was a time when I'd have jumped in with both fists soon as someone dropped a fucking choc-ice.

…

Not so much now.

MONA: You've mellowed.

GERRY: Not really. I've just worked out where to put the anger.

…

Some fights aren't worth it. Aren't even fights, really.

Pause.

MONA: So we'll just leave it at that.

GERRY: Will we?

MONA: As something that happened. And didn't do any harm.

GERRY: Yeah.

...

It doesn't mean we can't –

MONA: No of course it doesn't. That'd be good.

GERRY: Good.

MONA: Are you OK?

GERRY: Would it make any difference if I wasn't?

AMY and ANDY on the harbour wall.

AMY: This is about the size of it, sitting here

You're a spark in all this bigness

This roaring bigness over the horizon

It's what people come for, now

Have always come for it, although

They'll tell you, and be right

They found ways to live with it, work it

To survive it and survive in it

But really, what happened when they saw it was

They didn't stop and turn around, go back

Beaten by its vastness like spooked animals

They could have, but they didn't

They fell spellbound into fascination, and

To enough of them, the ones that stayed

The bigness said, this is home, not too many

And not too few, it said to them

This is where we make our stand

And they were transfixed, and on the headlands

They built monuments to Gods, then God

And fixed the heavens, the date of Easter

Wrangled out of monks and Kings and Rome

Trained those who sailed on that sea to view

The motion of the heavens, too, eclipses

Transits, the coasts of far flung islands

And also built the ships that got them there

They still build ships here

 State of the art, and turn out sailors here

With skills, transferable from trawler to tender

To ferry and to monstrous cargo-carrier

And send them out onto the global sea

Not just here, into these waters

We're apparently on the verge of taking back

But out across the globe because

That's what this globe-connected settlement

Has always done –

ANDY finishes his chips and screws the paper into a ball.

ANDY: Where's your chip paper?

AMY: In my pocket.

ANDY: Will you –

AMY: No fucking way.

ANDY: Well why does my coat have to smell of chips?

AMY: Shared responsibility.

Pause. ANDY takes a pair of heavy-duty pliers from his coat pocket, stuffs the chip paper in, puts the pliers back on top.

Andy.

ANDY: Yeah?

AMY: Was that a pair of pliers?

ANDY: In my pocket?

AMY: In your pocket.

ANDY: Yes it was.

AMY: Show me.

ANDY: You've seen them.

AMY: Show me.

MARK: I was the lad who went to sea

Who took the opportunity to

Live the life of ages past

But came to grief, was taken fast

I was the lad who went to sea

And now is only history, my

Lonely eyes with water fill, and

Every day I miss life still

I went because I couldn't find

The balance of a peaceful mind

On stable land, the rolling waves

Could help me leave the dark behind

GINNY: I spent a lot of time wondering who to blame. Felt like a lot of time, anyway.

…

It burned. It really kind of fucking… burned.

…

Weeks, definitely. I remember I started thinking about who to blame and by the time I'd come to, the season had changed. More light. Less. I can't remember. It's all a bit of a blur.

…

And I still didn't know. Who'd let him down. Or me. And then I realised it wasn't anyone. Or it was everyone.

AMY and ANDY are back at the Tourist Information Office.

AMY: It's been fun Andy. But I think this is getting beyond a joke.

ANDY: Think of it as a public utility.

AMY: Why are you doing this?

ANDY: Information. It's a public utility.

…

And so is human contact. My mother used to work here.

AMY: She doesn't any more though, does she?

ANDY: And you know what used to put her in a good mood?

AMY: Your mum hasn't been in a good mood since 1987.

ANDY: Human contact. She used to say she was a point of human contact.

AMY: Barely.

…

She slapped me round the back of the head once for talking while the telly was on.

ANDY: She was a different woman when she was at work.

…

I saw her. When I used to go in in the holidays. You know what she looked like? Pride. That's what she looked like. She knew the name of every place you could stay in this town and who owned it and whether they took dogs.

AMY: Well she had it all written down.

ANDY: She was like a human encyclopedia of Whitby. And what have we got now?

AMY: We've got phones now.

ANDY: It's not the same. That human contact. That way a place talks to the people who come to visit. Through the people who know it best. It's a public utility. It's a right.

AMY: It's a shame, in a lot of ways, Andy, that things have changed. But this isn't a bloody human rights issue.

ANDY: Why not?

…

Everything's a human rights issue.

AMY: Well a restaurant is human contact too, isn't it?

ANDY: It's not the same thing.

AMY: Look, Andy.

> …
>
> In some ways, I want things to stay the same as much as you do. I want us to do things the old ways. Look at the shop. But it's a different world now.
>
> …
>
> If we break in. What are we going to do?

ANDY: We're going to barricade ourselves inside.

AMY: And then what?

ANDY: Call the Gazette.

AMY: And say?

ANDY: Hang on.

> *ANDY takes a piece of paper from his pocket and unfolds it. He reads.*
>
> This is a statement on behalf of the Coalition for Historic Industries and their Preservation.

AMY: Christ.

ANDY: Good, isn't it? So. This is a statement on behalf of et cetera et cetera.

> …
>
> We are outraged –

AMY: Who's 'we'?

ANDY: You and me, initially.

AMY: Not on your fucking life.

ANDY: We are outraged at the decision, taken in complicity, no doubt, with Scarborough Borough Council, to throw our beloved Tourist Information Office to the ravening wolves of globalism.

AMY: The ravening –

ANDY: It goes on –

AMY: I'm sure it does.

ANDY: It does.

...

While it might be thought a small thing, this act of disobedience, it is part of a larger whole. Towns like ours stand or fall on their history. That history is what allows us to move forward. However, moving forward at the price of that history should be resisted at all costs.

AMY: Hasn't this already been decided?

ANDY: I'm getting to that. I'm getting to it.

...

We are a proud people, but we are also a welcoming people. We have, in our way, looked outward at every opportunity, while preserving our traditions. And this office has always been a port of call in stormy seas. A hand of welcome, come rain or shine, for those who wish, sometimes coming from so far away, to temporarily share that history with us. And now, having made so many momentous decisions, having chosen to preserve our independence, that which gives us a character of our own, worthy of the curiosity of others, we slam the door of welcome, and replace it with the same generic call of capital that echoes in a thousand other places. No more.

Pause.

AMY: Is that it?

ANDY: So far. I was thinking I could put a couple more hours in overnight.

…

Something about the bloody Algerinos selling us down the river.

AMY: I'm not sure you should be getting that parochial –

…

Also is this really a Scarborough problem?

ANDY: What isn't?

…

And then end with an inspirational quote, like –

…

'We are made fast to a mooring upon the wethering shore.'

…

You know. Captain Cook. We'll make ourselves fast to a mooring. Of principle. And also a literal one.

AMY: With what?

ANDY: I don't know. There's bound to be some gaffer tape or something.

AMY: In the hills above the town

Standing within glint of sea

The mines come, funded by promises

Dig the future from the ground

Twenty million tons a year of potash

From here to processing to China

Yet one more connection to stand with

Prawns and lobsters, vampires

Church calendars, the transit of Venus

And now trade deals, needed

Beyond the reclamation of the fishing grounds

Whatever that means in practice

But it was always the way for us

Backs to land, looking horizon-wards

Imagining new possibilities

Hidden by the curvature of the Earth

And these days, these uncertain days

We follow the commands of currents

More complex even than the ones

We learned to read on sea surface

Here is the cheapest place to get shells off

Here is the cheapest place to land fish

Here is the wind, on this sandbank

So we'll build the ever-swirling turbines

GINNY: I went up on the moors. Beyond where the Chinese
are going to put the potash mine. You know. The one

that's going to solve all our problems. Stood next to one of the wind turbines. Same as they're building out to sea.

…

The blades going round. Just revolving. Endlessly. You stare at them and this weird thing happens, Like you can't tell any more if they're being driven by the wind or they're driving it. Do you know what I mean? I thought the golf-balls were weird. All those Americans up the coast listening for death coming. Do you know they can hear people talking on mobile phones in Basra, or Aleppo? I thought that was weird enough. But these things. Imagine seeing one rising out of the sea. Imagine what he saw. I stood by one up on the moors and they make. They make just the most unearthly sound. Like some kind of creature stalking the land. Something that came down on a meteorite, like in a film. Fell out of space and then just standing there, flying round against a bright blue sky. Making this sound like it's lost. Like it wants to go home.

…

Imagine if it was the last thing he saw. Before he went under. Before the boat knocked him under.

…

Big wind turbine. Big wind turbine just revolving above his head. Making that sound. Last thing he saw, last thing he heard.

…

I dream about him, making that sound. Sitting on the bottom, making that sound. Opening his mouth and that sound coming out.

The arcade.

GERRY: I think about what happened.

…

I mean in here. Between us.

MONA: I thought I'd said –

GERRY: I'm not trying to make it happen again.

…

I'm just saying I think about it.

…

And I think it was about forgiveness. Not blame, maybe, but forgiveness.

MONA: I didn't need to be forgiven.

GERRY: I know the inquest said suicide.

MONA: That's what it was.

GERRY: It's true.

…

I wish I'd known him better, Mona.

MONA: We don't really know our kids though. Not the sum total of them.

GERRY: Maybe. Maybe what I mean is I wish he'd known me better.

MONA: He didn't drown himself because of you.

GERRY: I can't have made it easier.

…

It wasn't that –

…

It was the fact he couldn't tell me he was suffering.

MONA: He hid it.

GERRY: Let's –

…

Look, I can't do this. Let's talk about something else.

MARK: My loneliness led me to fall

Beyond the bounding harbour wall

I loved the boat, it anchored me

To know all its machinery

But loneliness, a different fall

Before a year had passed, the call

Of depths in sorrow, depths below

Became hypnotic undertow

I should have gone inland, too scared

Of what could lie there, I prepared

Trained for a life upon the sea

A failed escape from what I feared

AMY and ANDY inside the Tourist Information Office.

AMY: It's just a room, Andy.

ANDY: There's no such thing as just a room.

…

Could have done with a lick of paint anyway.

AMY: Andy, it's just an empty room now. They've pulled out the phone sockets. There's no light bulbs, even. There isn't anything left to save.

ANDY: It only looks that way if you've already given up.

AMY: It's a good job it is empty.

ANDY: Yeah. If it wasn't, then we'd *really* be too late.

AMY: Probably get done less for breaking into an empty building.

…

And if it was done out already, I wouldn't put it past you to take a piss in the sink or something.

ANDY: Why would I do that?

…

It's good though. We're in before they've properly got their claws in.

AMY: It's going to be a nice restaurant, Andy.

ANDY: It's not the wine list I have a problem with.

AMY: That's not the point.

ANDY: I'm not a fucking philistine.

AMY: I never said you were.

ANDY: That's it though, isn't it? I couldn't give a shit what they're cooking here. Or even if it's food.

AMY: What else would they be cooking?

ANDY: You know what I mean.

ANDY pulls a table to the centre of the room.

I just don't see why everything has to be –

AMY: It's a locally owned business. Just like mine. I used to work here Andy, and I got out and started my own shop.

ANDY: That's not the point is it? Not the point at all. Your place didn't take anything away. It added to it.

ANDY balances a chair on the table. He tests it for stability.

You think I don't know people have smartphones nowadays? You think I don't know there's a million different ways to find out where something is or what to do or where you're gonna stay when you get there?

ANDY unzips his coat and starts to pull what looks like a bed sheet out of it.

Not the point, is it? How many people live in this town?

AMY: I don't know. Let me fucking look it up.

ANDY: Fourteen thousand. Give or take. And fourteen fucking hundred years of history. Fourteen hundred fucking years of history, stuck out here on this little piece of land around a river mouth. And you're telling me we're so desperate. We're so desperate to participate, to be the same as everywhere else, that we close the one place down where you can interact with a human being. Someone who has knowledge of all that. Who can say, thanks for coming. This is who we are. This is our identity. Because we have computers to do that now, and we need to monetize every atom of space.

…

It's hardly special, is it? It's hardly capitalizing on what makes us special.

...

Give me a hand with this.

AMY: For fuck's sake. What's that?

ANDY: Banner.

AMY: The windows aren't big enough.

ANDY: It's not for the windows, is it?

Pause.

AMY: If you think I'm helping you get that on the fucking roof you can fuck off.

ANDY: All you need to do is hand it up to me.

...

I'll go up through the loft. They used to keep the spare stock up there. I bet there's five hundred Bram Stoker mugs up there still. I bet there's all sorts.

The office.

GERRY: So you said there's a lot wanting to train.

MONA: There's more wanting to sign up than ever. I don't know exactly what that means. It could be an indication, couldn't it that things are on the up. Here at least. That there's hope for something coming back.

GERRY: So that's great.

...

It's what you wanted.

MONA: I didn't vote for it, but it's what I wanted. If it actually happens.

GERRY: Unintended consequences. I voted for it. Not to save the fishing though. I thought that was long gone. I was just sick of being talked to like I was a prick.

MONA: I'm not saying it *has* been saved.

…

Just more people are hopeful about it than I would have expected.

GERRY: Like I said. Great.

…

But what?

Pause.

MONA: But I'm not sure if I want it back.

AMY, in the Tourist Information Office.

AMY: There's a tipping point sometimes

Between launch-pad and trap

This place lives on it, we totter

Between past and future

On the stutter between, this is enough

And the bright knowledge of the world

We wait, as if it was not our choice

To see if we will stay or leave

Whether our feet are planted

Or the town will not hold them

Like leaning into the cliff-edge wind

Beyond the ruined abbey walls

One version of us in the past

Another version leaping into space

Neither of those versions certain

There used to be certainty

And the town used to be big enough

We used to know in our bones

Our place in the world

Even when the sea was carved up

It was still a mark of territory

A familiar jurisdiction of the commons

Ours and theirs, here and there

But then the fires guttered out

Cottages sold for second homes

Standing empty half the year

Or even more, and the rent too much

And the boats guttered out

Eclipsed by bigger vessels

And the way the fishing rights got handled or

The indifference of machines to danger

But the knowledge didn't fade

It somehow stayed on

Enough of us here to feel distinct

Just far enough out to be bounded

There are still shadows of it

Bright shadows, but still shadows

We build boats too big to stay here

And we train all-comers for the sea

This place has enough history

To become its own museum

And fight it or embrace it

How we live in it is up to us

GERRY and MONA.

GERRY: Let's have that drink.

MONA: I'd love to. You know I would.

…

But I'm not going to.

MONA goes to leave. Pause.

When Mark killed himself, I thought of my granddad. His best mate, he told me. This is when I was only little, God knows what the hell he was thinking. But –

GERRY: It was a freak occurrence.

MONA: I know. But I could have seen it in him.

GERRY: He wasn't in his right mind/

MONA: My granddad/

GERRY: And went in, and sometimes you just can't save people.

MONA: He said when he was younger, and things weren't like they are now. There wasn't all the technology.

…

Sometimes they'd meet up, in the middle. The ships from here and the ships out of Denmark.

…

Sometimes they'd meet up, when the weather was good. Maybe they'd heard each other on the radio and wanted to say hello. Maybe they'd just come up on each other. But however they did it these crews would pull up alongside and they'd talk.

GERRY: Come and have a drink.

MONA: Turns out, back then, anyway, there was enough in both dialects they could understand each other. Sort of. They had more in common with each other, in the way they spoke, than they did with people in London or Copenhagen.

…

And my granddad said, one of these times, they were pulled up close to this Danish boat. Shouting across. And he was standing next to his best mate. And there was this one Danish lad. Probably about their age. And the way he used to tell it was, this lad just stood at the rail. Everyone was trying to communicate. Talking about the weather that was coming. Where they'd been. What the catch was like.

…

Except this one lad just stood at the rail. And he stared at my Granddad's mate. Wasn't shouting. Wasn't waving or smiling. Just stood there.

…

He said it was perfect calm that day. Blue sky. Starling's egg.

…

Anyway, they finish up. They have a drink together. Pour some whisky and toast each other and the Danish do the same. And they go on. They start their engines and as the boats are pulling away. This Danish lad. My granddad always said he was. Angelic. That's what he said. There was something about him that seemed on fire. He wasn't a man to ever use words like that.

…

This Danish lad waited until the boats were moving apart, and he shouted something across.

GERRY: Walk with me.

…

We don't have to talk.

MONA: He shouted across. You. Meaning my granddad's mate. You need to be careful. Your heart. Don't let it pull you in. Your heart's too heavy to be out here.

…

And he was right.

…

I wish I'd seen it in him.

GERRY takes MONA's hand.

GERRY: He was good at hiding it. I never saw it either.

The Tourist Information Office.

AMY: What the fuck are you doing?

ANDY shouts down from above.

ANDY: OK. Pass it up.

AMY climbs unsteadily on to the table and passes the bundled banner up to ANDY. Sounds from above, a window being forced open, some scrambling.

I'm out!

AMY: You're out of your fucking mind.

MARK: I walked these streets before I left

   I tried to find some joy to heft, the

   Pain I felt, its bursting power

   Destroyed that quest in silent hours

   I walked these streets before I left

   And understood the self-made theft

   Of life, dark one way, dark the other

   I left and then it tipped me over

   I should have gone inland, too scared

   Of what could lie there, I prepared

   Trained for a life upon the sea

   A failed escape from what I feared

AMY in the Tourist Information Office.

AMY: Andy. Will you come down from there.

ANDY: No.

AMY: Hang the banner and let's go.

ANDY: You know the banner's only part of it.

AMY: So you're going to stay up there all night?

ANDY: I'm going to stay up here for as long as it takes.

…

You knew what you signed on for.

AMY: I didn't sign on for anything.

…

You know what? Fuck you. I'm going home.

ANDY: Do me a favour and smash that chair up before you go. The table too.

AMY: Why the fuck would I do that?

ANDY: So they can't get up.

AMY: Good plan, assuming there's not a step ladder in the whole of fucking Whitby.

…

Andy?

…

ANDY: You don't have to stay, mate. I'm up here now.

AMY: Are you kidding?

…

What if I leave and you –

ANDY: I'm literally ten feet off the ground.

GINNY: I don't know why he did what he did.

   …

   Maybe it's not important, the why. Not as important as the doing of it. The fact it has been done. It becomes a fact and you have to deal with it because there's no going back.

   …

   My brother, on a boat, out in the North Sea. My brother makes a decision. My brother, drowning. My brother, drowned.

   …

   I'm not sure I ever want to leave this town again, if that's what happens to you.

   ANDY unfurls a banner. It reads – TOURISM IS HISTORY.

AMY: Andy.

   …

   Come down now, eh?

ANDY: Why would I do that?

GINNY: He's part of the history of here now. In the same way the actual history is.

   …

   As in, I can't help seeing him. I don't mean I actually see him.

MARK: But you do.

GINNY: But I do. Obviously. That's just a trick of the mind though.

   …

I don't go out much anymore.

ANDY: This is what we are now. A tourist town.

…

We shouldn't forget that. It's part of our history.

AMY: Who do you think's going to eat in this restaurant?

ANDY: Yes, but look at what it's replacing.

…

A sign. An office. It says, we care that you're here. You are important to us, and we have a stake in how you look at us.

GINNY: I've been up to St Mary's once since you died. Went up the hundred and ninety-nine steps, up above the east cliff. Took a bottle with me. It was a lovely day. Cold and empty. Didn't have a drink in the church.

…

Sat in one of the pews. One of the ones that says 'for strangers only'. Thought it might make me feel like a stranger.

…

Sat there and thought. This town is full of strangers. The ones that come from outside. To sit in the church. To hear about vampires. Or sea voyages. The real and the fictional. The wreck of the *Demeter* and the setting out of *Endeavour*.

…

Of course *Endeavour's* not a real ship. Not the one here now, anyway. But still.

…

Thought about the strangers who come here. How maybe there's no difference between coming here for history and coming here for fiction. They're both as real as each other. Both real reasons to come here.

ANDY: I just want something here that says – we know you're here to look at us.

AMY: There's plenty here that does that.

...

Pub's still open.

ANDY: I'm not coming down.

GINNY: And it's being worn away.

...

A few years ago, when the last big land-slip happened.

...

They've mostly stopped it now, so they say. But a few years ago, when the last big land-slip happened. Do you remember that?

MARK: Yeah. I remember it.

GINNY: You do?

MARK: Yeah.

GINNY: I miss you.

MARK: I know. I miss you too.

GINNY: Why did you go away?

MARK: I don't know for sure. But maybe –

...

I wanted to be part of something bigger than myself. I was scared of being trapped. On my own with myself. I thought the water might get rid of the fear.

GINNY: And did it?

MARK: It got rid of everything.

GINNY: So the cliff by St Mary's slipped away as the coast eroded, and it took part of the graveyard with it.

…

People's bones ended up on Henrietta Street.

ANDY: You could come up.

AMY: I think what you're doing is pointless.

ANDY: Then why help me then?

AMY: Because you're my friend, and I thought it might make you happy.

GINNY: More than nine hundred years there's been a church there.

…

Who knows whose bones they were.

…

I sat there in the church and thought about that, and about all that time slipping away down the cliff. And about how nobody can ever remember whose bones they were. But the lives. The bodies they used to be in, walking around. Those lives were the foundations of the story that brings people here.

…

Then I walked out into the graveyard. Far as I could. I had a drink then and I looked out at the sea and I poured a bit on the floor for you.

MARK: Thank you.

GINNY: You're welcome.

ANDY: You feel sorry for me.

AMY: No, I don't. I just think this place can survive the loss of a tourist information office.

GINNY: I guess that would have been the place to see you.

MARK: I'm not buried there.

GINNY: No, but maybe a light on the horizon.

…

But anyway. I stood there and thought about the bones sliding down into the street. How they were always there. Since they were put in the ground they've been there, suspended above the town. And suddenly there they were, in the street. Like history was suddenly in the wrong place.

…

And they re-buried them.

…

They made the cliff as safe as they could, and they re-buried the bones. Put them back in the churchyard.

…

I thought about that, and I thought about you, somewhere out under all that water. How your bones will never come back. But even if they're lost, you'll always come washing in, reminding me you used to be here. And that has fucked this place for me. But I don't want to be anywhere else.

MARK: I'm so sorry I left you.

…

I didn't leave you, anyway. Or even here. I just wanted to be somewhere else. But I couldn't imagine myself anywhere else at the same time.

AMY: If I come up there for five minutes, will you think about coming down?

ANDY: Will you think about staying up here?

GINNY: I'll always want to see you.

…

But if I'm going to stay here, I can't be looking for you any more.

ANDY and AMY sit on the roof of the Tourist Information Office.

AMY: You know they'll still come? Whatever this building is.

ANDY: I know. But it's heritage, isn't it?

AMY: Heritage.

ANDY: Coming here to look at the past. It's as much a tradition as the past you come to look at.

Boston

*A nature reserve near Boston, Lincolnshire. Mid-afternoon in May.
MARK, late twenties, is sitting on a bench outside a corrugated barn.
ANDRIUS, in his forties, is standing a short distance away.*

*NB – GINNY's verses in this scene are sung to the tune of the folk song
'The Lincolnshire Poacher'*

ANDRIUS: I'm sorry for disturbing you.

MARK: No. It's fine.

   …

   Always open to visitors.

ANDRIUS: And birds.

MARK: Well. One brings the other.

ANDRIUS: Yes.

MARK: The wetlands bring the birds. The birds bring the visitors.

ANDRIUS: No birds today.

MARK: Loads of them. You just have to get your eye in.

ANDRIUS: It's OK. I'm not here for that.

MARK: If you just want to take a walk around, that's fine.
   Some people just come for the solitude.

ANDRIUS: Yes.

   …

   My son was here, yesterday.

MARK: Right?

ANDRIUS: With his school.

MARK: Must have been yesterday morning. Only school group we had in.

…

Miss Morris.

ANDRIUS: You know her?

MARK: You get to know the teachers. Yeah. I know her. Ginny.

ANDRIUS: A good teacher.

MARK: She is. Loves the kids. We always have a good time. They're some of my favourite kids. The ones in her class.

…

Which one was he?

ANDRIUS: Which one?

MARK: Your son. What's his name?

ANDRIUS: George. He had a good time here.

MARK: Excellent. Did he leave something behind? A bag or something?

ANDRIUS: No. You showed him some owl shit.

MARK laughs.

MARK: Yeah. Well. No. Not really. Owl pellets. They're not exactly –

ANDRIUS: Owls don't shit? He said owl shit.

MARK: Well he wasn't.

…

It's probably my fault. Not that I would have used the world shit. Obviously. It's just hard to know if every kid understands.

ANDRIUS: He just made it up. He's like that. Likes to make up little things.

MARK: No. Owls shit. They absolutely do shit. But an owl pellet's not –

ANDRIUS: Good. It doesn't seem natural. For an animal not to shit.

MARK: Hang on.

MARK leaves. ANDRIUS stands. MARK comes back with an owl pellet.

Look.

MARK holds out the owl pellet. ANDRIUS takes it.

ANDRIUS: It's very dry.

MARK: Yeah. Not when they come out. But they dry out quite fast.

Pause. ANDRIUS holds the owl pellet in his hand, and looks at MARK.

Break it open.

…

Go on. See what's in it. Break it open.

ANDRIUS: With my fingers?

MARK: Yes. With your fingers.

…

You see what the owls do. Barn owls, these are. Although a lot of owls do it. Other species too. But what they do is, they can't digest bits of their prey. Bones, mainly. And if they were to pass through, they'd rip up their intestines. Like, properly shred their insides to bits. So the indigestible bits lie in their stomach for a few hours til everything useful's been absorbed and then. Up they come.

ANDRIUS has broken the owl pellet open with his fingers. He is staring into it.

Let's see what you've got there.

MARK comes to stand beside ANDRIUS and peers into his hands.

Wow. Lucky you.

ANDRIUS: Lucky?

MARK: This is a good one. Mind if I –

MARK reaches into ANDRIUS's hand and removes something carefully from the pellet. He delicately pulls away some pieces of pellet still left on it and holds it up in his palm.

You see that?

ANDRIUS peers into MARK's hand.

Mouse skull. She'll have swallowed him whole. Take it.

MARK transfers the mouse skull to ANDRIUS's palm.

It's even got the bottom jaw with some teeth still in it. Look. Don't often see that.

ANDRIUS stares into his hand.

ANDRIUS: I never knew this happened.

MARK: The digestive system of birds. Isn't something a lot of people think about, unless they shit on your car or your new coat.

ANDRIUS: True.

MARK: So he liked it here?

ANDRIUS: Who?

MARK: Your son. George. Yesterday. He enjoyed it?

ANDRIUS: Very much.

MARK: That's good to know. You should bring him again.

…

Next time you come. You can just turn up, you know. Well of course you know. You just did.

ANDRIUS: Yes.

MARK: So you should bring him.

ANDRIUS: He's dead.

Pause.

MARK: I'm sorry, did you just say –

ANDRIUS: He was in –

…

He died in an accident. Last night.

A primary school classroom in Boston.

GINNY: We live by light of a waxing moon

In a land so broad and flat

The trees stand tall when they stand at all

And the soil is rich and wet

The water's knocking at the gate

As warming seas do rise

And they come from foreign lands to work

The farms and factories

Yes they come from foreign lands to work

The farms and factories

An office near the Port in Boston. MONA is sitting at a desk. AMY sits opposite her, leaning back in her chair.

MONA: Did they think this was going to be a difficult conversation?

AMY: Nothing like that.

…

Someone from the paper needed to come down and talk to you. Might as well be me.

…

I said I'd so it. I'm not even sure they know we know each other.

MONA: Well. Been a while since we got to reminisce over our school days.

…

Hasn't it?

AMY: I'd be up for a bit of that. If you were.

Pause.

MONA: If it was anything to do with us, you know I'd be the first to/

AMY: I know. I'm just –

   …

   Loose ends.

   Pause.

MONA: He went in quite a way from here.

AMY: About half a mile up the Haven. Far end of the country park.

MONA: Captain of the Mareike saw him first.

AMY: Yeah. I'm hoping to talk to him.

MONA: Geert. He's a good guy.

AMY: Poor fucker. Got the kid out. Did his best but –

MONA: How long was he in there?

AMY: Not long. That's the worst. They think a few minutes earlier and it might have been a different story.

MONA: The Mareike was on the way in. High tide.

AMY: Not far off.

MONA: So he'll have gone in even further upstream and been carried this way.

AMY: He can't have been in long.

MONA: Do they think –

   …

   Anything about it that seems/

AMY: Don't know. It's public land. Nothing but fields on the other side. Nobody around. Not even dog walkers and there's usually one or two. The police are talking to the kid's friends. Seems like he might have been on his own.

MONA: How old?

AMY: Eleven.

MONA: Jesus. Jesus fucking Christ. Where were the parents?

AMY: Mum's away seeing family. On her way back now. Dad was at work.

MONA: And we're trying so hard to be polite

Professional, and neutral, though a boy died

Slipped into the river in the cold and almost-dark

An easy mistake on the muddy bank

Where he liked to stand and watch the boats

Thinking about who he was, a new being

Shaped by a people from an unknown country

Head full of foreign words and games

That felt out of place here, less real

Than the country he was born in and is part of.

And he's from where?

AMY: Lithuania.

MONA: Right.

AMY: The parents. The lad was born here.

The nature reserve. MARK and ANDRIUS are sitting outside the hut on a bench.

ANDRIUS: I'm sorry for coming here.

MARK: No. No. It's. I can understand why you'd want to –

   …

   I mean I can't. Understand. How you must be –

   …

   I'm sorry. I'm so sorry.

ANDRIUS: George.

MARK: George.

ANDRIUS: Jurgis. But we never called him that. Would have been Jurgis.

   …

   He loved school.

MARK: I bet he had a lot of friends.

ANDRIUS: A lot of friends.

   Pause.

   The police spoke to me.

MARK: I suppose that's normal.

   …

   Were they OK? The police. Not OK, but –

ANDRIUS: What could I tell them. He was doing what kids like to do.

MARK: Was he –

   …

   I'm sorry. What a stupid question.

ANDRIUS: What?

MARK: Was he on his own?

ANDRIUS: He liked it. Plenty of friends but he liked to go
   down to the river. Just an hour. Never in the dark. Was
   always back by dark.

The classroom. GINNY is at her desk.

GINNY picks up her phone, calls MARK.

MARK's phone rings. He looks at it. Cuts it off.

ANDRIUS: I'm sorry. I should go.

MARK: You shouldn't. Please. Take as long as you want.

ANDRIUS: You have things to do.

MARK: Really. Nothing that can't wait.

The classroom.

GINNY: They came in waves, they always have

   And pooled around the work

   The fields got picked and the bosses fat

   And true, some jobs they took

   The terraces and the caravans

   Were crammed with them in time

   But it's not their fault the wages paid

   Were slashed for the bottom line

   No it's not their fault the wages paid

   Were slashed for the bottom line

And some made money and went home

When they'd saved what they could

And others stayed and put down roots

Of family and blood

The numbers grew, the numbers shrank

The census always lied

And the kids grew up with accents

More ours than from outside

The kids grew up with accents

More ours than from outside

The nature reserve.

ANDRIUS: So much water here.

MARK: Not as much as there used to be.

…

We're letting it back in. The water. Re-wilding, it's called. Buying back unused agricultural land. Making it like it was before.

ANDRIUS: You can almost see the sea.

MARK: It used to be the sea. Connected to it, at least.

ANDRIUS: Maybe it will be again.

MARK: Well, now and again, maybe. When the tide fills the channels.

MONA: In a town this size opinions take root as facts

Because there are enough of us

We don't have to own the thoughts if we don't want to

More than we own any background noise

We can hide behind – some people think

Or – I'm just reporting what is said

And never have to stake a place to stand

So they become commonplaces

In local papers or around pub tables

Because we don't know everyone else here

We can reflect the darker thoughts

We don't claim any part of

The Port.

MONA: We've never had a problem.

AMY: I know.

MONA: Never had a problem with keeping people out.

AMY: I'm not suggesting –

…

It's unrelated.

MONA: We're a shipping port. It's a dangerous place. So we take steps to make sure nobody's here who isn't supposed to be.

AMY: The kid liked to come down and look at the ships, is all.

MONA: A lot of them do.

AMY: Liked to watch them coming in.

MONA: In case you hadn't noticed, there's a pretty big fence.

AMY: I'm in no way suggesting –

MONA: That we keep perfectly maintained for precisely this reason.

AMY: There's no way he could have gone in from your end.

...

The route from his house to where he went in goes nowhere near here.

MONA: So I don't really know why we're even part of the story.

AMY: You're not. Just background, like I said.

Pause.

MONA: What does the father do?

AMY: Runs his own business.

...

Came here as a farm-worker about twelve years ago. Now he's a plasterer.

MONA: He probably knows some of our lads.

AMY: The Lithuanians?

MONA: Through the community. Bound to.

AMY: How many have you got?

MONA: Six. Everyone else is local.

...

None of this is on the record.

AMY: Of course.

...

Like I said, just tying up loose ends.

…

Excuse to see you, really. Been ages.

MONA: What are you going to write?

AMY: That it's what it is. A fucking tragedy.

MONA: You know what's going to happen.

AMY: Yeah.

MONA: The problem with this town is it's small enough that everyone feels like they own it and big enough for the arseholes to be anonymous.

…

People don't dislike each other any more. They just dislike types. If I'm honest we could do with a bit more personal animosity.

AMY: Different for the kids.

MONA: I guess. The kids are better at it.

…

Your letters page is going to be a fucking nightmare. Website. Comments box. Whatever.

…

They let their kids run wild. They don't know our ways.

AMY: We're here to give a platform to the full variety of local viewpoints.

MONA: Yeah. Funny how that works.

AMY: A kid fell in the river. Hard to see how anyone could make that a political issue.

MONA: You know that's not true.

The nature reserve.

ANDRIUS: You have kids?

MARK: Me. No. Not yet.

ANDRIUS: Are you married?

MARK: No.

ANDRIUS: I don't know what I'm going to do.

MARK: I wish I could say something about that.

   …

   I wish I could help. All I can say is I met him and he was a good kid.

ANDRIUS: It's enough, maybe.

ANDRIUS pats MARK's leg.

   I think I need to go for a walk.

MARK: Do you want –

ANDRIUS: No.

ANDRIUS leaves. MARK's phone rings. He looks at the screen. Lets it ring. It stops. It rings again. He answers it.

GINNY: There's pubs some never go in

   And there's shops that some avoid

   On either side of any line

   Defences get deployed

   And we're not good with languages

   And they're just here for coin

There's a few out there who see the gap

But never see the join

Yes, always a few who'll see the gap

And never see the join

The Conservative Club bar in Boston. MARK enters. GERRY is sitting at the bar with a pint of bitter. It is early evening.

GERRY: Hello stranger.

MARK: You on your own?

GERRY: Left me in charge. You want a drink?

MARK: I'm OK.

Pause.

GERRY: Shame. About that lad.

…

It is.

…

I always said that bank's treacherous if you don't know what you're doing.

…

Always said that to you. Didn't I?

MARK: Been many in?

GERRY: The usual.

MARK: So not many.

GERRY:

Pause.

GERRY: Some vicar from the Stump came in, actually. One of them things. Curate.

MARK: Yeah?

GERRY: Wanted to drop off some leaflets. Non-denominational service.

MARK: Yeah.

GERRY: Community-minded. Aren't they?

…

MARK: Going to go?

GERRY: Ha. Fuck off.

MARK: Not your thing, is it?

GERRY: There's plenty it's still their thing.

MARK: You sure about that?

GERRY: Good luck to 'em. It's nice to see some community spirit.

MARK: This town's full of community.

GERRY: Well there's communities plural, and community like it used to mean.

MARK: Why do you still come here? Dying on its arse.

GERRY: Don't be so sure. Judo last night. Salsa dancing every Tuesday.

MARK: When's the last time you saw the MP in here? For a Conservative Club, it doesn't often get a visit from the local boss, does it?

GERRY: He's nobody's boss. Flash in the pan, that shithead. Never mind he looks all of twelve years old.

Pause.

MARK: How's Sonny doing since he got mugged?

GERRY: Sonny won't come here any more.

MARK: You been to see him?

GERRY: Been meaning to. See if he needs anything.

…

Surprised those fuckers didn't steal his tin leg.

MARK: They know who did it?

GERRY: Everyone knows who fucking did it. The man's coming up eighty years old. I know what I'd like to do if I got hold of them. Not that anything'll happen, even if they find out who did it. 'Course they won't. Nobody who knows anything is going to talk, no matter how many council interpreters we have to pay for.

MARK: You need anything doing? Round the house?

GERRY: You just stick to your birds. I can sort myself out.

MARK: You need anything?

GERRY: I don't need any help, if that's what you're asking.

MARK: How are the neighbours?

GERRY: They keep the drive spotless. Immaculate. Power-wash it every weekend.

MARK: You want to watch it. They'll put you to shame.

GERRY: Got a window-box too. Can't say we've had much conversation. The kid seems nice enough. Clean. Maybe he'll even speak the language.

MARK: I see kids like that every day. They speak the language fine.

GERRY: Well they don't to me.

    …

What you doing here?

MARK: I don't know.

GERRY: Bollocks.

GINNY: The votes came in, were counted out

    The pubs rang loud with pride

    But the change they thought they'd cried out for

    Was trying to stop the tide

    And the tide doesn't care for your own small voice

    While it makes its ebbs and flows

    And the people you blame for your problems, they

    Don't magically go home

    No, the people you blame for your problems, they

    Don't magically go home

MARK: You used to never see me, did you? One day to the next?

GERRY: You've got your life, I've got mine.

MARK: Not now. Back then. I used to wander all over the place.

GERRY: Was a different world.

MARK: It wasn't that long ago.

    …

But you let me, didn't you?

GERRY: Let you what?

MARK: Wander around. It's just part of being a kid. I used to go down to the river and all that.

GERRY: I often wonder.

MARK: Things weren't really that different

GERRY: If I hadn't bought you those binoculars for Christmas that one year. No idea why I did it, even.

  …

If I'd known. Fucking birdwatching.

MARK: You never worried did you?

GERRY: If I hadn't got them for you, you might have ended up somewhere else.

MARK: Dad.

GERRY: What?

MARK: Did you worry about me?

GERRY: Down by the river? No I credited you with a bit of sense. Enough not to fall in anyway.

  …

Didn't have enough sense to get out of this place though, did you?

The Port.

AMY: How's Andrew's Polish coming?

MONA: Better than mine. But then that's what they say. Best way to be bilingual is learn both languages at once.

Pause.

AMY: You know if it had been up to me –

MONA: Please.

AMY: No, I want to say it –

MONA: We've been over this.

AMY: We've never really been over it though have we?

   …

   Not really been over it. I know there's a lot of stuff you probably want to say to me. And it's fine. It really is. And I think I should –

MONA: You knew him, Amy.

   …

   That's what fucking gets me. You fucking knew him. More than that, you fucking liked him. You were at our wedding. You turned up to the registry office. You danced with his fucking uncle. You were sick in the fucking car park.

AMY: I'll take your word for that.

MONA: You fucking were. All down the side of the fucking ticket machine.

   …

   Piotr put you in a fucking taxi.

AMY: I know he did.

MONA: He's a good man.

AMY: I know he is.

MONA: Really? Because it didn't seem like it when you put his picture in the fucking paper.

AMY: It was the best picture we had.

   The Conservative Club.

GERRY: So how are things out there?

…

You going to flood us again?

MARK: If we re-wild the fens, then it's actually less likely –

…

You know, I'm not doing this again.

GERRY: It's OK. I know.

MARK: You talk as if I don't know people need to eat.

…

What do you think the game-plan is, Dad? Flood centuries' worth of farmland so the country runs out of fucking veg? It's a tiny project on unviable farmland.

GERRY: I used to be able to stand on a street corner after school, and they'd come and get you for a few hours' picking, and it was a decent wage.

MARK: That happens to other people now. I'd have thought you'd be glad about that.

GERRY: I'll be glad when young lads from round here can learn to do it again. When the wages go back up, that's what's going to happen too.

MARK: You're dreaming.

GERRY: I'm a bloody realist. You're the one dreaming, son. You can't say on one hand we need every inch we can to grow food and on the other say we need people bringing in to pick it. If we're crowded enough to need all that land then we've got enough local labour to work on it, given the right employment conditions.

MARK: Sonny went to Germany in the 60s. Worked as a bricklayer. He wasn't the only one.

GERRY: He was a good one too. There were jobs over there and he went.

MARK: So what's the difference?

GERRY: You think the Germans welcomed those lads with open arms? And the difference is if he didn't work, he didn't get paid. And if he asked for anything he didn't get it. Off you go and don't let the door hit your arse on the way out of the country. They had the right idea about migrant labour. Here for a reason, and when the job's done, thanks, here's your wages, sod off home.

Pause.

Tidal power. That's what we need. All across the wash. That's what your birds are in the way of.

MARK: Jesus Christ.

GERRY: Do I think you're going to flood the farms? No. But bloody hell you're looking us backwards, not forwards. I thought I was supposed to be stuck in the past.

MARK: It's always a pleasure to see you. You know that?

The Port.

MONA: A fucking epidemic.

AMY: That's not how we put it.

MONA: Get involved in the discussion and have your say.

AMY: That's just the standard wording.

MONA: An epidemic of drink driving. Like it was infectious.

AMY: That's not how we meant it.

MONA: That's how it sounded to the people who put notes through our letterbox calling me a traitor for having a Polish husband.

…

Could you not have said something, Amy? Could you not have said, I know that bloke? He's decent. Don't make him stand in for everyone who fucks up. Use a different photo.

AMY: But he did fuck up, didn't he?

MONA: It was the morning after his birthday.

AMY: So?

MONA: I'm not saying he was right. I'm not saying he shouldn't have gone to court, or been suspended. But he was so fucking marginal they had to re-test him. And you made him the poster boy for everyone who drinks a bottle of fucking vodka and decides to go for a joyride.

AMY: It was the only decent photo we had on file. The story was very clear it wasn't about him specifically.

MONA: You think anyone actually read the story?

AMY: There wasn't anything untrue in it.

MONA: Yeah but there's the truth you tell and the truth people hear, isn't there.

The Conservative Club. GERRY is preparing to leave. He puts a large bunch of keys down on the table.

GERRY: You know where everything is.

MARK: It's been a long fucking day.

GERRY: I bet it has.

…

You just need to lock up. Back. Front top and bottom locks. Set the alarm. You can drop the keys through the letterbox. I'm fucking done.

MARK: You're kidding.

GERRY: Take some responsibility, eh?

MARK: It's not my fucking job.

GERRY: Oh and switch off the fruit machine. Don't know why we bother switching it on to be honest. Last time they came to collect there was four fifty in the tray and two quid of that was pre-decimal.

GERRY struggles into his coat.

Keys through the letterbox. Don't worry about waking me up. I'll be dead to the world.

MARK: Just do it now. I'll drive you home.

GERRY: I think you can handle the responsibility son. Your world now. Don't worry about tidying up. Cleaner's coming in the morning.

MARK: Where's she from?

GERRY: What?

MARK: The cleaner. Where's she from?

GERRY: Fuck off.

GERRY turns to leave. GINNY arrives.

Sorry love. We're shut. Should have been here twenty years ago. It was thriving.

GINNY: Hi Gerry.

GERRY: Oh, it's you.

GINNY: You OK, Mark?

GERRY: Thought you had better things to do than mess around with him.

GINNY: Probably do, but I'm here.

…

You weren't at your place. Came to see if you were OK.

MARK: How did you know I was here?

GINNY: I'd looked everywhere else. Just a last thought on my way home.

GERRY: Right. Well.

…

Condom machine's broken.

MARK: Fuck off Dad, if you're going.

GINNY: I'll see you Gerry.

GERRY leaves.

You OK?

MARK: Are you?

…

I'm sorry. Must be fucking awful.

GINNY: They tell you at college it's going to happen. And you never think it will. Not really. But you know it might.

…

I'm going to have to do a –

…

There'll be an assembly in the morning. I don't know why
I'm here instead of thinking about what to –

MARK: Come here.

GINNY: Fucking hell Mark. Fucking hell.

MARK and GINNY hug. It's awkward but welcome.

The Port.

AMY: I'm sorry.

MONA: Well that's a bit too little a bit fucking late.

Pause.

AMY: Mona you know I –

…

I admire you. After everything. It must be –

…

I guess. The uncertainty. But it's going to be OK.

MONA: There isn't the least bit of uncertainty, and if there
was, it wouldn't be my fault.

…

I made my decision about where I stood. It wasn't me
who sat on the sidelines writing copy that I didn't believe
in to try and please people I didn't fucking agree with.

AMY: I don't get to choose what people think.

MONA: You get to choose what you do about it.

AMY: I guess I'll see you.

MONA: The kid was born here, by the way. Local.

AMY: I know.

   …

   I know that.

MONA: I wonder if you're going to write it though.

   AMY leaves.

   Outside ANDRIUS's house. GERRY is drunk.

ANDRIUS: Did something happen.

GERRY: I'm fine. I'm fine.

ANDRIUS: You're bleeding.

GERRY: Fell over.

ANDRIUS: You're drunk.

GERRY: I've had a drink.

ANDRIUS: It doesn't matter.

GERRY: I just need to get home.

   …

   I'll be alright once I get home.

ANDRIUS: I'll help you. Do you have keys?

GERRY: Course I've got keys. For my own house. Course I've got keys for my own house.

   …

   Let me have a sit down. Don't make me move too fast.

ANDRIUS: I won't make you do anything. I can wait. I've got time.

GERRY: Where you from?

ANDRIUS: I live next door to you/

GERRY: Doesn't matter. I don't care.

> …

> Doesn't matter anymore.

ANDRIUS: Let me get you some water from the house.

GERRY: No. No. I just need a rest.

> …

> You're a good lad. See me through the window, did you?

ANDRIUS: I was on the step. Smoking.

GERRY: I was never allowed to smoke in the house either. Not after we had the kid.

> …

> Never got out of the habit. I still have the odd fag on the back step.

ANDRIUS: I know.

GERRY: He's not lived with me for years. Some things don't change.

ANDRIUS: Can you get up?

GERRY: Give us a minute.

> *GERRY tries to get up. Fails.*

> Give us a minute.

> *Pause.*

ANDRIUS: Where have you been?

GERRY: Just down the club.

ANDRIUS: Was it fun?

GERRY: No. God no. I don't go for fun.

> …

> Used to be on the council. You know. Used to be on the council. Wouldn't have let this happen.

> …

> Voted off because some silly cunt decided to stand against me. You know why?

ANDRIUS: No.

GERRY: Everyone went hysterical for a fucking bypass. Like that's the only issue.

> …

> You know the bypass?

ANDRIUS: No.

GERRY: Exactly.

> …

> We had bigger problems. But everybody wanted a fucking bypass. Bigger problems, you know?

ANDRIUS: You want to try and get up now?

GERRY: I was just trying to put things right. Fair deal. You know. For everyone.

ANDRIUS: Ha.

> …

> Well. I would have voted for you.

GERRY: Not sure about that.

Pause.

Kid drowned in the river yesterday.

…

It's a fucking tragedy.

Pause. ANDRIUS helps GERRY up.

You know where he was from?

ANDRIUS: He had blue eyes.

GERRY: What?

ANDRIUS: Blue eyes. His mum too. I don't know what I'm
going to say to her.

Pause.

One night, I look in his room. He's awake. It's late. But
he's awake. Out of bed. He's looking through the gap in
the curtain. Through the windows.

GERRY: Who?

ANDRIUS: My son.

GERRY: I've seen him.

ANDRIUS: He was looking out. And I said, why aren't you in
bed? And he said Dad, you should help him. I went over.
Looked out of the window too. You were sitting on our
garden wall. You looked OK. Drunk. Like now. But OK.

…

I've seen a lot of that kind of drunk. Funny. When
someone drinks enough, you can't tell, really, where
they're from.

GERRY: I don't remember.

ANDRIUS: You were sitting on the wall, with your head in your hands. And he said, he looks sad about something. You should help him. Maybe he can't get up. And I said. I said he's probably sad about a lot of things. I can't help him with that. He looks OK. He looks like he'll be OK. And he said it again. You should help him. And I said. You know. The things he's worried about, they'll change. He'll probably be fine.

…

Go to bed, now.

…

He wasn't from the same place as me.

GERRY: Where was he from?

ANDRIUS: Here.

GERRY: You're not from here.

ANDRIUS: No. I'm not.

…

The kid, though. He was from here.

GERRY: Can I go in? I need to go in.

ANDRIUS: Yes. Of course.

ANDRIUS starts to help GERRY walk towards his house.

GERRY: Need to. Need to call someone.

ANDRIUS: Are you OK?

GERRY: Just. I think. I think maybe I need to sit down and call someone.

ANDRIUS: I'll help you. It's fine. I'm here. I'll help you.

The Port.

MONA: And this is one of those clear, so clear

It's painful, one of those uses

Of dead kid as metaphor for something

It has to be, doesn't it?

The kid dies in the river, and, we're

Supposed to think of him as symbol

Born of two cultures, working together

He drowned in the place he belonged to

And we're pointed not towards

His humanity itself, but the human links

He represented, of their washing away

In a tide not even those who called it

Into being could see coming.

And the cold death in the river

Becomes more, a severing of

Ties, and a stilled hope floating

On a tide that is not just water

But the rising and falling of

Thought and truth and lies.

We're always told we're a symbol

Of something our country needs

Or something it is failing to do

But a dead kid in the river

Is a dead kid in the river, let

Him be that, let him just, this once

Be one of ours.

The Conservative Club. MARK and GINNY look at each other.

MARK: What are you going to do?

GINNY: Go home. I just needed –

…

Something. I needed that.

MARK: Would have thought you had better places to get it.

GINNY: Not tonight.

MARK: You can stay.

GINNY: Here?

MARK: At mine.

Pause.

I don't mean. Just. If you want to.

GINNY: What good's that going to do?

MARK: You can have the bed. I'll stay on –

GINNY: No, Mark. I mean. Thanks. But no.

Pause.

Have you had a drink?

MARK: Maybe a couple.

GINNY: Fucking hell.

MARK: Different, these days.

GINNY: Always is, when you go back to it, isn't it? Always going to be different.

MARK: I can feel it.

GINNY: I bet you –

…

Jesus. I'll drive you home.

MARK: I've only had –

GINNY: I'll drive you home. Lock up. You can pick up your car in the morning.

MARK: I need to drop the keys.

GINNY: It's on the way. It's fine.

MARK: It's different this time.

Pause.

GINNY: I hope it is, for your sake. Doesn't matter to me any more. Come on.

GERRY's house. ANDRIUS and GERRY have just come in.

ANDRIUS: You going to be alright now?

…

You want some water? I could get you some water.

GERRY: Have a drink with me.

ANDRIUS: No. But I'll get you some water.

GERRY: Why won't you have a drink with me?

ANDRIUS: It's not a good idea.

GERRY: I want another drink.

ANDRIUS: You got any?

GERRY: Plenty.

ANDRIUS: You'll be OK then. Enjoy yourself.

GERRY: Shouldn't we get to know each other?

ANDRIUS: Maybe. Not tonight. I don't drink.

>   *Pause.*

GERRY: Fair enough. Fair enough.

ANDRIUS: I'll go now.

GERRY: Fetch me the Scotch from the cupboard, eh?

ANDRIUS: You should do that yourself, if you want it.

GERRY: Fuck you, then. Think you're so special you can go
    and fuck yourself.

>   *ANDRIUS turns to GERRY. Thinks better of it. Turns to go. MARK*
>   *walks in with the keys. ANDRIUS and MARK look at each other. A*
>   *moment of recognition and confusion.*

MARK: Dad?

ANDRIUS: I helped him in from the street. I was just going.

MARK: How are you –

ANDRIUS: I live next door.

>   …

>   This is your father?

MARK: Yeah.

ANDRIUS: He's very drunk.

Pause.

Thank you for today. Earlier. I'm going to bed.

GERRY: Mark, will you fetch me the Scotch?

MARK: Do you need –

ANDRIUS: No. Thank you. He should drink some water.

ANDRIUS leaves. GERRY tries to get up. Sits.

GERRY: What are you doing here?

MARK: Bought your keys back.

MARK puts the keys on the table.

You should go to bed.

GERRY: Get the Scotch, have a drink with me.

MARK: I've got a lift waiting.

Pause. MARK gets a bottle of Scotch and two glasses. He pours a large amount of Scotch into both of them and hands one to GERRY.

GERRY: She'll wait.

MARK: Really?

GERRY: Your mum always waited.

MARK: No she didn't Dad, she fucking left.

GERRY: You've got a bit of rope yet.

MARK: We split up six months ago.

GERRY: She's outside, isn't she?

Pause. MARK drinks most of his Scotch.

MARK: That's me done, Dad. I'm off home to bed.

GERRY: Mark.

MARK: Don't sleep down here.

...

Fuck it. Do, if you want. I don't care.

GERRY: You knew that bloke.

MARK: He's your next door neighbour.

GERRY: You haven't been round here since he moved in.

MARK: His son came to the Reserve yesterday. School trip.

GERRY: Came along, did he? Normally they let the kids run
wild.

Pause.

Well maybe not him. He's nice enough I suppose.

*GINNY enters. She watches MARK and GERRY. MARK pours himself
another Scotch, and one for GERRY.*

GINNY: Mark.

MARK: Started now.

GERRY: There's no stopping him, love. There never was me.

...

Least that's one thing I gave you eh?

...

I'll have to go round. Thank him. He's not so bad.

172

MARK: Just leave him alone Dad. Let him get on with what he needs to do.

GERRY: Maybe there's been a bit much of that, eh? Maybe it's time to stop leaving people to their own fucking devices.

MARK takes the bottle. Walks behind GERRY. Takes a swig, then gently pulls back GERRY's head and pours the rest of the bottle into his mouth. MARK puts the empty bottle down. GERRY swallows. Starts to gag slightly.

MARK: Come on, Dad.

MARK helps GERRY up and leads him gently out of the room. Sound of GERRY throwing up in the bathroom. Sound of MARK helping GERRY upstairs.

GINNY: The votes came in, were counted out

The pubs rang loud with pride

But the change they thought they'd cried out for

Was trying to stop the tide

And the tide doesn't care for your own small voice

While it makes its ebbs and flows

And the people you blame for your problems, they

Don't magically go home

No, the people you blame for your problems, they

Don't magically go home

They stay and buy the house next door

They do the jobs you did

They have trouble with the census forms

They stay and raise their kids

The kids survive, or most do

And they speak just like our own

They forget they're supposed to be different

In the only place they've known

They forget they're supposed to be different

In the only place they've known

MARK enters.

MARK: Used to do that when I was a teenager. Sometimes it was the only way to get him to shut the fuck up and go to bed.

GINNY: Happy now?

MARK: Of course I'm not fucking happy.

…

Listen to me.

GINNY: I'm listening.

MARK: Out there. The sea used to come in. On the high tides. The spring tide. Like fucking clockwork. Inundate the whole thing. All the low ground from here, miles inland. The birds. Migrating birds. Stopped off and. They used to rest here. On the channels. And guys on flat-bottomed boats would lie in wait. You ever seen the pictures?

GINNY: Of course I've seen the pictures. You showed me the pictures.

MARK: They'd lie in wait with these massive fucking nets, and just. Herd. Herd the birds towards them. All working together and when they took off, they'd all fly, the birds, the whole flock, into these nets and then they'd be caught. And when they drained the fens. For the farmland. For the cabbages and the carrots and the brussels fucking sprouts, they stopped being able to catch the birds. But of course they'd taken away the other thing too. The water. The water the birds needed to rest on and to live. So the men fucked off and the birds fucked off, and now it's vegetables as far as the eye can see and they come here to pick them and sometimes their kids drown in the water that's left, and nobody gives a shit. And if they go home and it's just us. You. Me. My fucking dad and the vegetables. I don't know if I'm up for that. I really don't know if I'm up for that. And if the upside of everyone going back to where they came from is that nobody sells weird meat with unpronounceable names on West Street any more. Not that it'll happen. But if it does. That's not really enough of a fucking upside for me. You can't change things back by magic and some things you can't change back at all.

…

There's a tiny bit of that, though. The fens and the birds, that I can try and make come back. Just to say. The old and the new. They can exist together.

GINNY: I know they can, love.

MARK: Maybe it's too fucking late for that though, eh? Things have changed.

…

Is it such a bad thing?

Pause.

What was he like?

Pause.

The kid. George. Jurgis.

GINNY: George.

MARK: George. What was he like?

Pause.

GINNY: He was just a kid, Mark.

…

An ordinary kid.

MARK: That's all.

GINNY: That's all. That's the only thing I can say about him.

…

Sometimes that's all there is.

Stoke-on-Trent

A peal of church bells. All six characters are ringing. They are practised, enjoying themselves, in sync with each other. Sudden darkness and silence.

MONA: A place with a six-town sense of itself

Where you live among the relics

Of the glory of the past

And you wonder what it means

And you wonder where it went

And it's hard to get the sense of any

Future coming fast

And you know you're gonna be misunderstood

Cos you aren't like other places

And you don't fit in their rules

And you do your best to fill the gaps

Ripped open by uncaring hands

You know you'll never do enough to

Stop up all the wounds

NB – MONA's verses in this scene are to the tune (or at least the rhythm) of 'Punk is Dead' by Crass

A ceramics workshop in a redeveloped building in Longton. GINNY comes in with a tray of glazed ceramic mugs. She drops them, deliberately, one by one into a metal bucket, smashing them.

ANDY stands at the gates of a church. He is holding half a loaf of bread in one hand, and a half-bottle of vodka in the other. He alternates bits of the bread with swigs of the vodka.

MARK: There's always bread

If you know where to look for it

Nobody starves, not yet anyway

The community-minded make it

And they like to give it out

Artists make it, and they'll

Swap it for a story, sometimes

Even bakers make it, although

It's harder to get it off the bakers

Because they have to make a living

There's always booze

If you know how to pay for it

And that's easy, there's always

Someone who owes you a favour

Or someone who'll lend you a fiver

Or someone who'll share it for

You sharing yours down the line

You can even just take it

Just take it and run as a last resort

There's a solution for everything

The studio. GINNY tips the broken pieces of the mugs onto a table.

The belfry in Stoke Minster. GERRY is setting out books on a circle of benches. Bell ropes are tied away at the edge of the space.

MONA: So everybody's trying, everyone who gives a fuck

Could be marathon, museum

Or some leaflets, a parade

Or selling off cheap housing

To revitalise a street

Could be church or council, mosque or shop

To get a difference made

But one or two will always be the ones get left behind

When the skill-set gets to changing

And computers replace sweat

When the terraces get flattened

And the ones that don't get sold

For a quid a go and promises

To clean them up a bit

There's bound to be a bit of back and forth on either side

A frank exchange of views

On what we lose and what we keep

When a town tries reinvention

And takes stock of what it means

To plant one foot in its history

But take a forward leap

The studio. GINNY is working with the pottery fragments, laying them out on the table. ANDY enters. A moment of stillness.

GINNY: I think you're in the wrong place mate.

ANDY: Door was open. I'm sorry.

…

Didn't mean to scare you.

GINNY: You haven't scared me.

ANDY: I'm not on the rob.

GINNY: Nothing worth taking in here.

ANDY: I was just having a look in the yard.

GINNY: Be my guest. It's not my yard.

Pause.

This is where I work, mate. I'm working.

ANDY: You haven't got –

GINNY: No I haven't/

ANDY: I'm not asking for/

GINNY: There's tea money in the biscuit tin by the kettle.

…

Probably a fiver. Something like that. You can have that if you like.

ANDY takes the vodka bottle from his pocket.

ANDY: You want some of this?

GINNY: No, thanks.

ANDY takes a sip and returns the vodka to his pocket.

ANDY: What are you doing?

GINNY: Are you not from round here?

ANDY: No. I mean. What are you doing here on your own.

GINNY: I said. I work here. It's my business.

ANDY: Sorry. I was being nosy.

GINNY: No. This. It's my business. The business I own.

ANDY: Right.

    …

    Don't worry. I'm not/

GINNY: I wouldn't be worried if you were. Even if I couldn't beat you in a straight fight, which I totally could, there are about fifteen objects within reach I'd be able to completely fuck you up with. Not including this stuff right in front of me.

ANDY: Wow. OK. I wasn't –

GINNY: I'm pretty sure you weren't, but best to be clear.

    …

    Have a look round.

ANDY: Is there any tea?

GINNY: Fridge is broken. No milk.

ANDY: I could have it black.

GINNY: Kettle's fucked as well.

ANDY looks round the workshop.

ANDY: Oh.

   ...

So what do you do here, then?

MONA: Houses for a quid get snapped up fast as you'd expect

If you've got a full time job

And no other property, but

I'm not sure the neighbourhood

Comes out on top in that

When the folk who do the places up

Weren't there originally

The belfry. GERRY and AMY.

AMY: You haven't started yet.

GERRY: No. Still ten minutes or so.

AMY: Many coming?

GERRY: Depends.

   ...

Usually a full peal. Probably less this week.

Pause.

You joining us?

AMY: Got a meeting.

GERRY: Figures.

AMY: You of all people should know how many meetings there are.

GERRY: I'm out of all that.

Pause.

What you here for? Some tips? How to get elected as a party member in a town suspicious of parties. You'll be OK. You're Labour. Independents know our place round here and it's not in Westminster, apparently.

AMY: I'm not here for advice.

GERRY: Good, cos I haven't got any.

AMY: Wanted to tell you I got the house.

GERRY: Well congratu-fucking-lations.

AMY: We're in a church.

GERRY: We're in a belfry.

Pause.

I'm pleased for you.

AMY: No you're fucking not.

GERRY: Hey. We're in a church.

MONA: We had a rule when we started. Back in the 80s. You know. When we had the kind of enemies that at least made you hopeful. When if they were fucking your community up, at least it felt personal. Like you meant something to the people doing it. They could see you.

…

I have to get used to saying it. You don't remember the 80s. Most of the people I work with now were kids or they weren't here at all.

…

They do not fully remember the 80s. And fuck does it make me feel old.

…

Anyway. We had this rule. And simply put, it was this – when we're working together, you can piss whenever you like.

…

I say that to people now and they don't get it at first. They think it's fucking ridiculous. But it's not. It's fucking fundamental.

…

I said it to this one lad and he said, what, you mean just go in the corner, or the bin or wherever? And I said no. Not wherever. *When*ever.

…

Basic rights. You think these days freedom is something to do with getting fuckers out of your reproductive system. And it is. It totally is. But to even get that far you've got to get the fuckers out of your bladder first. And your colon, obviously, but piss is a more palatable word than shit. You've got to realise that most jobs, it's not even a political thing, they first thing they control, the first thing they buy, is your right to expel waste from your fucking body.

…

So the first rule of a communal working environment was – you can piss whenever you like. As a basic economic freedom.

…

The liberation of urination.

…

Some bastard who you never even met dictating when you're allowed to let liquid flow out of your own body and how long you get to do it. In order that your value to them as a fucking commodity is maximised. And it doesn't matter if you're taking bets over the phone or putting bulldozers together.

…

That is the very definition of an oppressive system. Having your fucking bladder held hostage so someone else can have a swimming pool. Which, ironically, they can piss in whenever they want.

…

So piss whenever the fuck you like. You are both trusted to the job you need to do, and allowed the autonomy to do the other stuff you need to do. We're not children.

…

Should be a fundamental human right. Maybe with an exception for air traffic controllers. But I still have to say it.

The belfry.

GERRY: Well. Congratulations. On the house.

AMY: I'd love it if you meant that.

GERRY: Where is it?

AMY: Same street my Grandad lived in.

GERRY: You know in the 1970s Stoke got asked to take in the overspill from Manchester?

…

The Government said to Stoke, look, Manchester's only up the road, really. You're both industrial towns. We're basically the same. Maybe you could take some of them off their hands. Two thousand or so.

…

You know what Stoke said?

AMY: I'm going to go with no.

GERRY: Why?

AMY: Because Stoke wanted to protect its own. The people from Manchester would have been at the top of the housing list.

GERRY: That's only part of it.

…

Stoke and Manchester aren't 'basically the same'. We're not interchangeable with anywhere else.

…

You can't just move people here and expect them to understand.

…

That's why we've always had so many independents on the council. Stoke hasn't imported the bullshit from the rest of the country because it doesn't work the same way. There's a different relationship between industry and art. Between the centre and the outskirts. Between politics in here and politics out there.

…

And now here you are, coming back, wanting to represent us. And buying your house for fuck all as a symbol of commitment to that, when it isn't. When what you're actually buying into is an attempt to drag us somewhere we don't want to be. Another dormitory town for Manchester or Birmingham. A fucking node on an integrated transport network with a few independent art spaces thrown in on top, so we can pretend we're attracting the kind of people who like independent art spaces.

…

You can barely get a bus from one end of this city to the other. Six towns that barely talk to each other when they have more in common than they do with anywhere outside. Never mind the bits that don't actually fit into the six towns. Be nice if we could fix that before we start going on about our convenient location with regard to the motorway system.

The studio. GINNY and ANDY.

ANDY: Why did you come here?

GINNY: What's that supposed to mean?

…

I live here.

GINNY hands ANDY a cup of tea. He lifts the cup to look underneath.

GINNY: It's one of mine.

ANDY: You work with any lithographers?

GINNY: It's mostly hand-painted.

ANDY: My mum was a lithographer. Dudson's. Forty years putting transfers on cups.

GINNY: It's a bit more involved than that.

ANDY: What would you fucking know?

GINNY: It's skilled work, lithography.

ANDY: It's a skill.

GINNY: I know. I just said. I know that.

    Pause. ANDY inspects the cup.

ANDY: Who buys these?

GINNY: People. To drink out of.

ANDY: I mean who do you supply to?

GINNY: Lot of online customers. Couple of shops.

ANDY: Big orders?

GINNY: No. Big enough.

ANDY: Like who, then?

GINNY: Selfridges.

ANDY: That's nice.

GINNY: Some places in Hanley.

ANDY: Oh aye. The new places.

    …

    Wood-fired pizza. There's a couple now that do wood-fired pizza.

    …

    Is it those?

GINNY: One of them, I think.

ANDY: That's enough, is it?

GINNY: Keeps a few people in work.

ANDY: A few.

GINNY: Would you rather I wasn't here?

ANDY: I'd rather there was a few more people involved.

GINNY: There's still mass-production. All over the city.

ANDY: Funny definition of 'mass'. Didn't realise it meant 'a tiny fraction of what there used to be'.

Pause.

GINNY: Guess I want to get a handle on what part of this you think is my fault.

ANDY: When did you move here?

GINNY: Uni. Eighteen. University. Never left.

ANDY indicates the broken ceramics on the bench.

ANDY: What's that?

GINNY: Just trying to work something out.

ANDY: What?

The belfry. GERRY and AMY.

AMY: You know what I can't understand?

…

I can't understand why you're not a racist. Not like you wouldn't have had company.

GERRY: Why the fuck would I want that kind of company?

AMY: Stoke for the Potters. Nobody understands us. We elect independent councils and we don't do national politics, so if you don't like that, don't come here.

…

You could so easily have ended up as a pub fascist and
yet the first time I met you you were handing out leaflets
about a drop-in centre for refugees.

GERRY: Of course I was.

…

It's not the ones who come here from further away that
are the problem. They get it. It's a blank slate. It's the ones
who come from closer to home and think they know how
it works.

MARK: This place grew along a coal seam

And I guess we came to it pretty late

This idea that identity and industry

Can tie together fragments, and we

Never really left it, if we're honest

The cottage, and the worker in the cottage

The raw ground-stuff and the artistry

Existing together under one roof

The dirty hands that lift the clay

Being the same hands moulding delicately

Or patterning precisely, that idea

Was at the heart of us, in a way

That other places didn't really fathom

Six towns grown first, then merged

Inventing their own working

As the cottages stuck together

Began to look more like factories

Again, not the mills of other places

But places for the gathering of specialists

Each pair of hands now a particular skill

And that's been our strength and our undoing

We came to solidarity late, collective action

All those powers seemed foreign

Not natural, given our solo origins

We found other ways of doing, founded

In our six identities, instead of across

The definitions of our labour

But also, we looked out, the finesse

The expertise that made us famous

Known more in China than by neighbours

Or sipped from in the furthest reaches

Of Empire, dark as that was

We looked outward over our neighbours

The world brought the six towns together

And the six towns looked at the world

AMY: I thought you might be pleased. That there might be a
   Stoke MP living in streets her family came from.

…

I thought that kind of thing was important to you.

GERRY: Not like this. I never voted for it when I was on the Council and I still wouldn't now.

AMY: Maybe that's why you got voted out, then. Maybe you were out of step.

GERRY: Maybe I still fucking am. There were a lot of things I was glad I was out of step with.

…

How's the campaign?

AMY: You've not been reading the Sentinel, then? Local girl makes comeback.

GERRY: Tend to avoid it, these days.

AMY: I think I'm going OK. You know how it is. Never can tell, can you? Of course a national campaign's different to a council one.

GERRY: Bigger stage, less power.

AMY: That's the problem, isn't it. You always thought anyone with the temerity to try and connect with the rest of the country was a fucking parasite.

GERRY: If it hadn't been for the rest of the country we wouldn't be selling off perfectly good housing stock for a quid to people who could afford to pay the market price.

AMY: It's an expression of commitment to the community I'm from.

GERRY: It's cynical, and that scheme wasn't meant for people like you to take advantage of. Or it shouldn't have been.

…

You've done alright. You should pay what you can afford.

AMY: I want to live here, and I want to help. And you know what I'm doing with the money.

GERRY: Yeah I saw. Giving some of what you save on mortgage payments to a women's refuge. Smart move.

AMY: You can't argue with that.

GERRY: Morally, no. But I'll give you this as well. It's fucking good politics.

…

It's not what you're spending your money on. It's what you're buying into.

…

I tell you though, you're right about one thing. And I bet you're finding it out.

…

There is a difference between local and national. Between fighting for what's best for this place because you stayed, or trying to make it like everywhere else because you left.

AMY: You think someone who's never lived here would understand it better?

GERRY: No. But I'm disappointed the kid who used to help me push leaflets through doors ended up thinking like you do.

AMY: Tell me what all those leaflets achieved then.

GERRY: They kept us out of national politics.

AMY: Is that what you told yourself while you were rubbing shoulders with fascists? That them getting on the council was the price of you keeping out of national politics?

GERRY: They're not there now, are they? Came and went.

AMY: And what changed? What did you buy with the independence? Couple of call centres?

…

Is that what standing apart looks like?

…

Or does it look like a man pissing his life away while he hides in a church?

GERRY: It's a belfry.

…

Don't come back here and tell me this place would work any better if London told it what was fucking good for it. You don't understand it any better than they do.

Pause.

AMY: Teach me.

GERRY: What?

AMY: Before the rest get here. Give me a quick lesson.

GERRY: Piss off.

AMY: You've been doing this for what? Thirty years?

GERRY: Thirty-four.

AMY: So teach me. I know there's more to it than pulling a rope.

GERRY: There's a lot more to it than that.

AMY goes to sit by a bell rope. Crosses her legs.

AMY: Show me what I need to do.

Pause. GERRY brings a box over.

GERRY: Well first, you never cross your legs in a bell tower.
    Both feet on the floor. At all times.

AMY puts her feet on the floor.

AMY: Bad luck, is it?

GERRY: It is if the rope catches your fucking foot.

GERRY puts the box in front of the bell rope.

Stand on this.

*AMY stands on the box. The rope dangles in front of her. GERRY
stands behind her.*

Put your hands here and here.

AMY puts her hands on the rope. GERRY puts his hands over hers.

Now. Don't pull too hard. It's not so much about force. It's
    about when you catch hold, and when you let go.

AMY: Is this –

GERRY: Nice and loose. You're a bit tense.

GERRY and AMY pull the rope. The bell tolls.

Right, and let go. And as it comes back up, grab it. And
    then bring it down.

AMY: You can feel the weight.

GERRY: Don't worry about the weight. The bell's ringing
    itself. All you can do it help it. You just need to give it
    some energy at the right point. Not too much. Just to keep
    the whole thing working. And let go –

…

And back on.

AMY rings the bell a couple more times until GERRY grabs the rope and brings it gently to a standstill.

AMY: Wow.

GERRY: How did that feel?

AMY: Not like I expected.

GERRY: You're a natural.

The studio. GINNY and ANDY. ANDY has pulled a chair up to the work bench. His vodka bottle is on the bench. He is concentrating fully on GINNY, who is laying out the broken ceramic pieces in front of him.

ANDY: So these were the bad ones?

GINNY: Not really. It's not about –

…

There are a lot of thoughts, yeah, a lot of schools of thought that are about trying to find the beauty in imperfection. Which is I guess the kind of thing you're talking about. Or how you fix something broken and you make it more beautiful. Kintsugi. That's one of the names for it, anyway. That's when you fill in the cracks with gold.

…

This is a bit different. These were perfectly good.

ANDY picks up a broken piece.

Careful.

ANDY stares at it in fascination.

Andy. Hey Andy.

ANDY puts the piece back on the bench.

ANDY: Sorry.

GINNY: No. Just. Be careful. It's fucking sharp.

ANDY: Do you never cut yourself?

GINNY: It's no problem if you're careful.

ANDY: So you just put them back together.

GINNY: Kind of. It's a thing I'm trying.

…

I want to mess about with. What happens when the breaking is deliberate.

ANDY: And then you glue them back together.

GINNY: No. I mean that'd be just. Fixing it, I guess. Wouldn't it.

ANDY: Just like before but not as good.

GINNY: I want to see what happens if you use the same –

…

The same bits or whatever. What happens when you find other patterns in them.

ANDY: They'll be useless though.

GINNY: For what they were for originally, yeah. But there's a lot of cups in the world.

ANDY: There's a lot of broken pots too.

GINNY: Yeah, but –

…

I don't know,

ANDY: It's not. I'm not saying I don't appreciate the value of art –

…

Sometimes it's all a thing needs. To be a thing. I get that.

GINNY: I don't think this is art, though.

ANDY: Therapy? Cos that's good too. When it's available.

GINNY: Not that, either.

Pause.

ANDY: What, then?

Pause.

Am I sitting a bit close? Do you want me to –

GINNY: No, it's fine. You're fine.

…

You don't get much control over how things break. I think that's what interests me. I mean you can –

…

You can take a mug, a cup, whatever, and you can drop it. Or you can throw it. You can choose the height, I guess. And how hard. And what you throw it in. Use a fucking hammer. I don't know. A million ways. But even if you control everything you can, there's ten million more things. Factors. That you can't be aware of, can you? You don't know what's inside it. Actually in the material. The tiny faults from variations in heat or where and when it got touched. You don't know about how it's going to spin. What's going to affect it when it's falling. What the world's going to do to it. How you're feeling when you do it. How you don't even know you're feeling when you do it.

…

The push and the pull.

ANDY: Are you sure this isn't helping you with something?

GINNY: I'm just interested.

ANDY finishes the vodka.

You polished that off.

ANDY: There's always more somewhere.

Pause.

GINNY: Why do you think you –

ANDY: Don't be a dick.

Pause.

GINNY: There's probably a beer in the fridge over there.

ANDY: Thought you said it was broken.

GINNY: Didn't say it'd be cold.

ANDY goes over to the fridge. Opens it.

ANDY: There's two. You want one?

GINNY: I'm OK.

ANDY comes back to his seat with a beer. Opens it. Drinks.

ANDY: Yeah it's a bit fucking warm but it'll do.

GINNY stares at the work bench.

You got someone?

GINNY: Have you?

ANDY: No. Too much like hard work.

…

I mean. I'm too much like hard work. I wouldn't mind,
but I can see why you wouldn't want to put the effort in.

…

Not you, obviously. Why one wouldn't want to.

ANDY looks at the bench. Points to two shards.

I'd say. This bit. And this bit. To start.

GINNY: Why?

ANDY: Something about the edges.

GINNY puts the two pieces next to each other.

Call it instinct.

GINNY: If you like.

ANDY: Pretty much all I've got left.

MARK: We're not emblematic of anything

I think there's a problem in perception

With a place this size, that doesn't

Look like a city, six towns threaded

According to the needs of dead processes

Along an artificial waterway

When you put it like that

It explains the geography, but still

It's a hard thing to get your head around

So people try to make you mean something

So they can make sense of you –

A symbol of failed industry, or

Inward-looking, immigrant expelling

Last redoubt of some mythic whiteness –

And maybe there are some here

Who believe that's the story they're living

But they're few and far between

We're more misunderstood

Than we're misunderstanding

We're more looked at than we're seen.

The belfry. GERRY and AMY. AMY is picking up the basics. She rings the bell several times. She lets it come to a stop. Silence.

GERRY: Bit more practice, you could be good at this.

AMY: Maybe I'll come every week if things work out at the by-election.

Pause.

Would you let me do that?

GERRY: I think about that lass a lot. The one who got shot on the way to her constituency meeting.

AMY: I didn't really know her.

GERRY: She seemed really dedicated.

AMY: I know.

GERRY: People are going to be even more angry. If things don't get better…

…

I worry.

Pause.

AMY: There's no need for you to worry.

GERRY: Right.

AMY: The guy was ill, Gerry.

GERRY: So they say.

AMY: He's not typical. He's not even typical of people who hold those views.

GERRY: There's a lot of people encouraged to hold those views.

…

I was independent. You're party. You're not going to be able to do dodge responsibility for stupid decisions at a national level.

AMY: At least with me there's somebody who cares about the area.

GERRY: Do you, though?

…

Cos from some angles you look like a fucking careerist.

AMY: So what if I am?

GERRY: Not a fighter.

AMY: I can be both.

Pause.

Always meant to ask you something,

GERRY: Yeah?

AMY: What's an atheist doing as a bell ringer?

GERRY: Who says I'm an atheist?

AMY: You don't believe in God any more than I do. Never been able to resist a pulpit though, have you?

GERRY: You ever heard of a tower grab?

…

I was about fifteen. Walking past here. Going to get the bus to see Crass play, at Syd's. This bunch of old fellas come practically running out of the church. Towards the bus station. About my dad's age at least. Wouldn't think much of it except they looked more excited than I did about spitting on Steve Ignorant. Turns out we're getting the same bus, and I sit near them. Ask them what's going on. I mean I must have been curious cos I was a shy kid for all the safety pins holding my trousers together.

…

Well a tower grab is when you spend a day in an area going to as many towers as you can, ringing the peals, and moving on. Only ones you haven't done before.

AMY: Collecting them.

GERRY: Exactly. I don't know, It just tickled me, more than anything.

…

Ended up in Christchurch once. New Zealand. These were the days you couldn't just hop on a plane on a whim, either.

AMY: How'd you afford that?

GERRY: Half price tickets. There was an offer.

GERRY laughs.

I saw it in the Daily fucking Mail. Can you believe that? Only bit of good those bastards ever did.

…

That tower came down when they had the earthquake a few years ago.

AMY: Stuff gets rebuilt.

…

It's about time we took our heads out of our arses and rejoined the rest of the country. We're too big to feel this fucking alone.

GERRY: What do you want from me? Your mind's already made up.

AMY: I want you onside.

GERRY: You want a cheap house.

AMY: It's an expression of faith.

GERRY: There's cheap houses in Bentilee. That'd be an expression of faith.

AMY: You think where I'm going to live will be easier?

GERRY: Honestly? Yes. Before long. Because there'll be easier people living there. People like you. And that's the wrong kind of change.

Pause.

AMY: Come to a meeting Gerry. Stop hiding. You don't have to cheer if you don't want to. But at least be open to the possibility someone who left here might still give a shit when they come back.

MONA: There's a price for independence, and it's being understood

Because we're not like the others

And we do things our own way

The solutions we get offered

They don't fit us like they should

But the way we talk about them

Means we have to play their game

The studio. GINNY and ANDY, facing each other over the bench. They are working silently, constructing something, each taking turns to choose a piece. They do this for a long time.

GINNY: You OK?

ANDY: You know what?

…

Surprisingly, yeah.

GINNY: Surprisingly?

ANDY: I honestly –

…

This is the kind of thing that'd normally do my head in. But it isn't.

GINNY: I know what you mean.

ANDY: Do you?

Pause.

GINNY: I think so. Like –

   …

   Like, when I first decided to do this.

ANDY: The Japanese thing?

GINNY: No. All of it.

   …

   It was like I had all these –

   …

   I knew how to do bits of life. And work. But nobody ever told me how to find somewhere to be. Handle money. Not actual money but business stuff. And people tried to help me. But actually in the end I had to find my own way. I just left uni and I was a bit. Lost.

   …

   It all felt a bit. Random. You know?

   …

   I guess I had to do the same thing.

Pause. ANDY puts the fragment he's holding down on the bench. He looks at GINNY for a long time.

ANDY: Is that meant to –

ANDY gestures to the bench.

   I mean.

   …

   Really?

GINNY: I'm just saying –

ANDY laughs.

ANDY: Fuck's sake.

ANDY picks up another fragment. Puts it down.

Fuck's sake.

…

Are you trying to teach me something? Is that what this is?

GINNY: Don't be daft.

ANDY: Do you know how many people used to work in a building this size?

Pause.

Are you trying to make this fucking *symbolic*? You and me, sitting here, gluing shit together like two fucking nursery kids? Supposed to find a life lesson in that, am I? Something I haven't already thought about?

GINNY: No.

ANDY: Is that why people like you are coming here? To help people like me?

GINNY: No.

ANDY: I didn't think so.

GINNY: I'll tell you something though.

…

It's certainly not for the fucking warm welcome.

ANDY: You can have a warm welcome, or you can have cheap rent. Make a fucking choice.

Pause. ANDY and GINNY laugh.

MONA: I'm working with a group of people at the moment.
On this thing called the growing project.

…

There's a girl I work with. I don't think she's ever left
Stoke before.

…

Maybe she never will. Doesn't matter. What I remember
is. It was the first plot we made. On the site of an old
pot bank, not far from Etruria as it happens. Where
it all started. Everything that makes us so special and
everything that's put us in the mess we're in. And –

…

You can be as cynical as you like about his, by the way.
I'm just giving you permission.

…

We did all the groundwork. Dug in the soil. Put some beds
in. Can't even remember what we planted. But we went
one day, and it had just started to come up.

…

She fucking cried.

…

And I'm thinking. Fucking hell, surely she's seen fucking
plants grow before. She's not crying over basic botany?

…

Of course she isn't. She's crying because it was the first
time in her life she'd made something happen.

…

She'd grown up closed off. No power. Doesn't know what she's smoking half the time. Never left Stoke. Barely even been to Newcastle. Living on a sofa and shitting herself in case she ends up in a tent in the park and someone threatens her with a thousand pound fine she can't pay.

…

You know what people like her get told they can do? Nothing. They get told nothing. They just get shifted from wherever the money's going to where it isn't.

…

We just scratched the surface. Literally scratched away the surface and put something there and she got to make a change. On her own terms.

…

That's how she's going to get off her arse.

MARK: We're not here to romanticise the work

The stackers in the kilns, sweating

Burning their skin, the miners

Dragging the coal unwilling from the earth

The long hours stretched in slavery

Or the pride that came with it

Growing this small corner of the world

Into a powerhouse of utility and art

We're not here either to romanticise that pride

That black-lunged sooty, straight backed

Love of labour and the hands that wrought it

That still clings on in brick-humped skylines

Where artists find new homes like hermit crabs

But what I will say is, those things shaped the city

Literally shaped and stretched it so

It ended only able to understand itself

Because those things shaped minds too,

Even if you came here at a time after that time

The roots connect, allegiance to your town

Your one of six, and then, those towns combined

It's harder still, from here, to see outside

When you try and say what's good for us

There are enough of us to argue back

Even if we don't quite know what we're saying

There are enough of us here to argue back

GINNY and ANDY. They have constructed something between them on the bench. It isn't exactly a pot, and it isn't a piece of art. They look at the object.

ANDY: Well. It's not pretty. But it's there.

GINNY: It's a step.

…

Where are you going to –

ANDY: Oh it's alright. I'm going.

GINNY: I wasn't –

ANDY: I know you weren't.

…

I have to get back. I said I'd meet someone for a smoke. If they've got any. Assuming my stuff's still there. You don't know these days. But what's the alternative? Sit in a fucking tent all day so it doesn't get shifted?

GINNY: Right. Well.

…

I'm not sure how this is –

…

Look, if you wanted to try. What I mean is, I'm fairly often here. Of an evening. There might be stuff you can –

ANDY: Don't invent work where there's no work.

GINNY: I wasn't.

ANDY: You think I could be an artist?

GINNY: Anyone can –

ANDY: Don't.

…

I know what you're trying to say, but don't.

GINNY: What was I trying to say, then?

ANDY: That you're going to save me.

GINNY: I wasn't.

…

All I was saying was, you're good at this.

ANDY: I have potential.

GINNY: Yeah.

ANDY: If only I'd believe in myself.

…

Make the most of myself.

GINNY: I didn't ask you to walk in here.

ANDY: No, you didn't.

…

Who asked *you* to walk in here, though?

GINNY: Nobody.

ANDY: Not anyone I know, anyway.

Pause.

GINNY: You know what? I think you should go.

ANDY: Don't worry. It'll be like I was never here.

…

Out of sight, out of fucking mind, eh?

MARK: Shelved and glittering exclusive objects

Art, that's built on shadows of the past

The hard lessons of historic industry

Turned into technique, dirt to heritage

Tendrils shooting from mass production

Into the workshops of fascinated artisans

I've got no problem with all that

I just suspect it might not save us on its own

Old limbs repurposed for a modern age

And from the outside, schemes and projects

Thrown into us by hands that want to help

But find it hard to grasp our shape

We look like you, but we're not really you

That not us saying – we don't want you here

We've always been connected to the world

How could anything work otherwise

But the world's solutions don't fit us

And our memories of smoke and glory

Are just that, smoke and memories

ANDY and MARK. Several months later. A café/bar.

MARK: How've you been?

ANDY: I've been alright.

…

I've been worse.

MARK: You've been worse, have you?

Pause.

ANDY: Yeah.

MARK: Drink?

ANDY: Yeah.

MARK: You going to pay me?

ANDY: No.

MARK makes ANDY a tea.

MARK: Well tea's all you're getting.

ANDY: Tea's all I want.

MARK: Makes a change.

Pause.

ANDY: I haven't had a drink in three months.

MARK: Good for you.

ANDY: Honestly.

MARK: I believe you.

…

Go on then. Why?

Pause.

ANDY: I don't know.

…

I do know.

MARK: Bail conditions?

ANDY: Not exactly.

MARK: It's just –

ANDY: I like tea –

MARK: Have you been in a bit of bother?

Pause.

Have you?

ANDY: Who told you that?

MARK: Who tells anyone anything?

Pause.

ANDY: Here to meet someone.

MARK: Yeah?

ANDY: Yeah.

MARK: They got any money have they?

ANDY: Imagine so.

MARK: Cos I don't mind you being in here. You know that. But it's not –

ANDY: They'll have money –

MARK: It's not a drop-in centre. It's a café.

ANDY: It's empty.

MARK: It's early.

Pause.

ANDY: When is it ever busy?

ANDY points to a poster.

Spoken word night?

…

Does it get busy on the spoken word night?

MARK: Yeah it does, actually.

ANDY: I bet it does.

MARK: Do you want to drink your tea and then fuck off, or do you just want to fuck off?

ANDY: I'm just taking the piss.

MARK: I know you're taking the fucking piss.

ANDY: Stoke-en word.

…

Should have called it that.

MARK: I actually thought of calling it that.

ANDY: Yeah? Why didn't you call it that, then?

MARK: Cos it's not fucking funny.

ANDY: I didn't think it was funny.

MARK: What did you think it was, then?

AMDY: Clever.

MARK: It's not that either.

Pause.

You should come down.

ANDY: I don't think it's my thing.

MARK: Suit yourself.

Pause. ANDY gestures to a record player in the corner.

ANDY: Vinyl records.

MARK: Yeah.

ANDY: Funny how they've come back.

MARK: People like the sound.

ANDY: Does it work? That record player?

MARK: Yeah.

ANDY: Lot of trouble though, aren't they?

MARK: I guess that's the point.

   …

   Not trouble. Effort.

ANDY: Same thing.

MARK: Completely different thing.

   …

   Difference between coffee and instant coffee.

ANDY: Same effect.

MARK: Same purpose. Different effect. I opened this place because I thought there'd be enough people here that'd understand that.

   …

   Also I thought Stoke was fucking boring and I wanted it to be less boring.

ANDY: Why didn't you just move to Manchester?

MARK: I tried that. It was shit.

   …

   Who are you meeting?

GINNY enters.

ANDY: Alright.

   …

   Long time no see.

MARK: Alright Gin.

   …

   You know him?

GINNY: Yeah. We've met.

MARK: Small world.

GINNY: Not really.

MARK: Coffee?

GINNY: Yeah. Ta.

   GINNY sits with ANDY.

   Hi.

ANDY: Hi.

   Pause.

GINNY: It's nice to see you again.

ANDY: So you got my note.

GINNY: Obviously.

ANDY: I pushed it under the door.

GINNY: Yeah. I mean not all the way. So half of it was wet.
And I've got a letterbox. But. Yeah. You did.

   MARK brings GINNY a coffee.

   Thanks mate.

MARK: You alright?

    Pause.

GINNY: Yeah. It's fine.

MARK: Right.

    MARK leaves.

ANDY: You busy?

GINNY: Always.

    …

    You?

ANDY: Not really.

    …

    Still gluing shit together?

GINNY: In my spare time.

    Pause.

ANDY: I'm sorry.

GINNY: What for?

ANDY: Being a prick.

GINNY: You weren't.

    …

    You could definitely have been more of a prick.

ANDY: No, hang on.

GINNY: You weren't.

ANDY: It's called making amends. I have to do it.

Pause.

It's step eight.

GINNY: But you didn't –

…

Look, mate. We met once. And it was fine. If anything I'm sorry I was –

…

I mean I'm not making assumptions. But there must be people you need to apologise to more than you need to apologise to me.

ANDY: Yeah, there are. Of course there are. But it's not about the size of the –

…

It's about what it meant. You offered me something and I –

…

It's about putting shit back together. You understand.

Pause.

GINNY: OK. Go on, then.

Pause.

ANDY: Sometimes, you feel like everything's so fucked, there's no point even trying to make things different.

…

There's been a lot of people in my life who've tried to help. And some of them have been dickheads, but most of them have been good. And a lot of them have been trying to deal with things they can't control. And sometimes I've not taken the help because it hasn't been the right time. Or there are factors out of my control. And sometimes I've been my own worst enemy.

…

But my sponsor asked me a while ago about people I rejected. Who might not have done things the right way, but were still. They were still trying to help a situation. And some of those people, I don't know where they are, and some of them are too far away. But I thought of you.

…

I don't know. So you're standing in for some other people. For a whole fucking history. Which must be weird I guess, but someone needs to do it.

…

So I'm sorry. And if you need anything. Let me know.

Pause.

GINNY: Yeah. Well. Apology accepted.

…

And I'm glad you're doing it. Whatever this is.

Pause.

ANDY: If you want to. If I was passing. I could –

…

I'm not saying you need help. But what you were doing that night. I've thought about it a lot.

…

Anyway.

…

I know you're busy. You should get on.

Pause. GINNY drains her coffee cup. Holds it out. Drops it on the floor. It breaks.

Manchester

When a place gets big enough
To tell itself a story
About mills and canals
And actually a Roman fort, (if you remember
Right at the start of this there was a Roman fort
In a place much smaller)
When a place gets big enough
To tell itself a story
And then big enough
To listen to its story, and believe it

A place, this place, might tell itself
A story about unity
A unity it likes to think about
As something spun here and world-spanning
Spun from a massacre of democrats,
Or woven tight around a bassline
And crime and drugs
And friendliness and violence
Warped and wefted, threads
From community and politics
From activism and a kind of anti-everything
The revolutionaries working in hotels
And the communists skulking in the library
Or pacing the factories they ran
Building theory from the screaming machines
Which, once invented, drew the labour here
Theory from the broken bones of the young
The hovel-housed, disposable bones
Of those who would otherwise
Have been born in cleaner country air
Or not born at all, if not born to serve
Those un-cherished by the owners

Of the machines they tended
As those owners raked the profits
And built them into stone-faced buildings
And spoke in those buildings
About their righteous moral duty
To improve the worker's lot
While denying those workers the autonomy
To speak about the ways
They thought their lot might be improved
And the place might tell a story
About how the workers found their voice
And set an example that resounds
Still to this day across the world

When a place is big enough
It might tell a story about the ways
The world would be different
If the place had not existed
About the invention of the computer
And the splitting of the atom
And the invention of community
And the invention of immigration
And the invention of welcome
And the rejection of slavery
About the love of love
And about the right to love
And the love of ourselves
The love of our resilience
The love of ourselves as tolerant
And standing for no one
And standing for nothing
That is imposed on us
We can be crushed, we say
We can be drugged, or starved
Of resources and community
And still, we tell ourselves

The world will see things our way
Because we have something it wants
That it cannot make on its own

When a place gets big enough
To have a concept of its north and south
Of the cardinal directions pointing
To differences in what we're like
The rich live here, the old rich,
And the new rich live here
And here, the recently arrived
And here the ones gone under
After the machines made them useless
So they will lash out, or buy instruments
Or have television programmes
Made about their essential dignity
And the modern ones here in the south
Who make those programmes
And here, the ones we said were welcome
And in the midst of it all
The ones we try to trust, except
We don't quite, we don't quite
Convince ourselves they fit
But we try, because we have said
We have said over and over
That we look out for each other here
And everyone is welcome

When a place gets big enough
To tell itself a story
And not only that, but
Tell itself a story it believes in
We hold rallies, we throng
For justice in the same wide space
That others thronged for justice
So many years before

And we take on the mantle
Of heroic defiance and togetherness

And we do this after an event
After the world has happened here
As we feared it might
And as we knew it would

We do this after a young man
World-poisoned and made hateful
Transforms himself to shattered dust
And takes our other children with him

And we tell ourselves
We will get through this
And we will, we do get through it
Because we always have
We get through it with dignity
And insects of industry carved in our skin
And with art and sport and music
We get through it quiet as neighbours
We get through it loud as love
With a smile in the street
With speaking out on the trams

But the thing itself. The young man
Looking through dead eyes
At a joyful throng before he flips the switch
That person in that moment
Is not a part of the story, is a thing
We cannot tell ourselves

When a place gets big enough
To tell itself a story
There are still things
That story cannot countenance

Cannot support without self-breaking
Under the weight it would be asked to bear

It's easy to overestimate the story
The binding effect of it
The loudness of it, when you're at the centre
Standing between those old buildings
Sheltering in record shops from the rain
Finding space in the empty mills
If there is any left, to make art
Putting new living space in old architecture
Or clearing ground for multicoloured slabs
Sealing in a modern way of living
It's easy to be swept up in the story
Looking at rows of bright windows
Watching them ranked from the train
Pulling in to the clean-edged centre
Filled with fast-lived life, sharp edges
And too many people to know

And it's too easy to hear that story
Take comfort, and believe it
In the warmth of refurbished terraces
Walls knocked through for light
Walls knocked through for space
Pastel coloured and hung
With block-print renderings
Of easy politics, reproduction slogans
Spray-painted on illustrated walls
Stencils of objects jostling
Vintage New York posters
The common reference points
Of a counter-culture, hidden
But not entirely forgotten
Under drifts of mortgage statements
And measuring the catchment area

Of well-regarded primary schools
And every object is a version
Of every other single object
From house to house to house
And we are media-literate
And concerned about the homeless
And all the pub-tables sanded
And thick-cut chips in metal baskets
And Christmas lights strung
Between shops selling tea pots
And subversive birthday cards

It's easy to hear the story
Resounding clearly, even in the places
Where money hasn't yet found flow
And regeneration is just a TV image
Even here it weaves through life
We see ourselves this way, brave
We see ourselves this way, dignified
Bound up in family and clan
In a way that feels as real
As the histories of ancient empires
Taking the establishment on
Surviving on wits, wiles and love
Listening to the part of the story
That runs joyfully outside the law
Breathless through alleyways
And in flat-roofed pubs

Or we hear the story a different way
In those same drained places
Setting jaws, determined
To make communities out of remnants
In boxing gyms and halls
Where we guide flying fists
And focus restless energies

Or pile up surplus tins
To make survival kits
For those whose fingertips are slipping
Because we will not let them fall

The story allows Gods too
For those that want their Gods
Amid the vanished grind of industry
The crushing weights lifted
Off and onto ships in inland docks
And later amid the server hum
The ergonomic chairs enfolding
The sculpted mouse mat wrist protector
The booze-slick pavement
The anonymity of weekend flats
There is room in the story for Gods
Fewer want them now, or would admit it
But all the world's Gods are still here
From the contemplative silence
In a meeting house, to the cathedral choir
From the temple to the synagogue
To recitation of the Friday prayers
And of course there are other borrowed Gods
Kidnapped from the East
To serve in suburban yoga studios
But part of the story is coming together
Part of the story is ritual, and belonging
And this still works, is still a strand of it

The story is of outsiders
Outsiders who become insiders
Because we know how welcoming we are
It's of holding out a hand
And boycotting cotton picked by slaves
Sacrificing comfort for solidarity
Nobody is from here if you go far back

A place created by the upsurge of industry
Can't claim roots as ancient
As some desert city or imperial capital
And perhaps there's a remembrance of that
In the way we see ourselves as open
It might not be true, but it's important
It's a hook to hang hope on
This idea the story includes the world
Places named after here on every continent
And the exchange of prices with Alexandria
Trade routes and the spread of our technology
Through our facility with raw material
We became the raw material of change
A beacon bending its light over horizons
Unafraid of the curvature of the Earth
Or the curvature of alien alphabets
Because there is a strength in the heart
That throws the arms wide, and says come in
But of course the story's felt
As much as it's told, and it's impossible
To tell a feeling like it was a history
There is a history here
And plenty of books to tell it
But history is a line, not a feeling
History doesn't cluster
Under the overhang of a department store
On the concrete apron of the loading bay
Desperate for companionship
Made aimless and sparking
Dependent on magic to get through the day
History does not leap bodily from the stage
Into a forest of sweat soaked arms
Or stand sentinel against drunks
Or sell Chinese factory plastic
Designed to distract kids on Market Street
History doesn't sit on benches

To take a rest from walking
Bent under heavy time, to supermarkets
It doesn't strip the roofs of disused pubs
Or infiltrate steel-gated alleyways
To try the locks of patio doors
History doesn't gather in churches
For three hour Catholic funerals
Live-streamed back to Jamaica
Or speculatively sell football shirts
In kid-thronged beer gardens
Celebrating victory in matches
Not even played until tomorrow
Story does that, story not marked
By dates known by all as turning points
But marked by category, each fact
Shared only by a few, but all
Points of light in the pattern of the whole
And the feel of the story's so fucking romantic
Not in a star-crossed lovers way
Although we have those too
But in the romance of authenticity
The coming from the streets
The swaggering non-conformity
Turn up at the house, kettle on
Eye-contact, mouth-corner
Openness of doors and hearts
That big, soppy dog-like sentiment
Of sounds that are not words
And palms grasping children's faces
Of easy touch, hand on shoulder
We don't kiss each other hello
Not much, and we don't hold hands
But we let weight rest on each other
We don't pull back at the warmth of touch
Quick to laugh, too, wide-faced and loud
We know there are exceptions

And get on the wrong side
Come harshly at us and ours
Things can turn rough quickly
But even that turn comes out of love
Out of the romance of protecting
Because the wider world might not
There is a sweet sentimental seam
That runs under 'our kid' like coal
Even runs under the gangster swagger
And the blue and red mentality
That awful fucking cliché we embrace
And even those of us who hate that cliché, mine it
Mine that seam based partly in the memory
Of actual mining, a camaraderie
Born in defunct pit-heads never known
But dimly alight in some shared image
As dirt streaked beacons of the love
We tell each other we so naturally bear
The story we tell is that we care
And we do, each in our own way
And all together, let's sing that song
And kid ourselves it means something
There's more to it than nonsense words
Thrown together to impersonate an anthem

That spectre of a truth once true
Commodified and packaged
Not just in ten thousand living rooms
But in hopeful new developments
Trumpeting their claim on banners
To a slice of glory and struggle
Wrapped carefully in stylish living
Fonts signed off in six hour meetings
To say with maximal efficiency
You can come home to this
It is a place you can feel as you live in it

This is an edge made safe
But kept just sharp enough
As you buzz yourself contentedly
Into stylish modern buildings that incorporate
The original period tiling

In a city this size, we create villages
Circles of knowing built to resemble
Some folk memory of the old ways
The boundaries of common land
The sounding range of church bells
The twists in vocabulary that say
You are not from here, we adapt these things
To work within a larger 'here'
Moving across membranes, thoughtlessly
The adaptable compounds that we are
Marking and re-marking the village boundary
From home to work to gig to art-class
Pub quiz to dealer to grey glass tower
Prison roof to glimpsed hilltop
To the weekends biking in the countryside
Or spent drugged and delirious
Or taking the kids to the football
Living in all these villages, being us

We are the ones who play guitars
We are the ones who smash windows
We shrink sleeping-bagged outside supermarkets
We take beginners' Spanish classes
We smile across parks of screaming toddlers
We comment effusively on each other's dogs
We walk in quiet pairs round galleries
We hand out leaflets witnessing Jehovah
We clear brick-choked canal basins
We worry about the DLA assessment process
We share binoculars to watch the planes come in

We volunteer to take the elders shopping
We run the woodland paths in skin-tight lycra
We curse or bless the ninety-second minute of the match
We cold-brew coffee, we worry about homework
We look at clothes we can't afford
We shoplift, we eat Chinatown noodles
We drink cocktails on the twenty-third floor
We smoke skunk in the underground car park
We write academic papers about heritage
We pontificate on the jagged edge of post-punk
We rehearse art and politics and theatre
We stand for mayor and try to house the homeless
We obliterate the crowd with backpack nailbombs

So, one day just before summer
On the anniversary of nothing significant
A young man wakes in the centre of the story
He drinks milk from the plastic bottle
His older brother bought from Morrisons
And puts it back in the fridge
Before, I don't know, praying
I don't know, but I guess it's what they do
And he sits for a while, the carpet is bad
Maybe that's it, how it started
Maybe he never lived in a place with nice carpets
He sits for a while, on rented furniture
One of a thousand ghosts the same chair has
Silently exchanged, one life for another
In this house alone, over so many years
He waits to feel special, part of something
The story of the city invisible to him
In a way it never used to be
Transformed into an absence, a darkness
Into which he will drop brief light
He sits, opens his laptop
Like a hundred people in the same room

Or versions of it, in that second
In lock-step with all of us
He opens the laptop and enters his world
Which he has trained to tell him
Exactly what he needs to hear
To speak to him in his own voice
Edged with the sweetness of authority
Sugar that says, this is smarter than you
Bigger than you, but this is yours
And these are your opinions
Over that, opens another window
Checks the event is still scheduled
The start time unchanged, the end
Perhaps he imagines the excitement of others
Checking this same schedule
Counting down the hours until lights up
Or the woman waking in a hotel, maybe
He knows two nights ago she was in Dublin
Maybe he doesn't think of her at all
And in an office high above the city
Where the currents of property
Are mapped, pored over
The life and death stakes of sailors' charts
Applied to hundredths of percentages
In fluctuating interest rates
The developers identify which sites to target
Structural integrity, internal supports
The computer generated image
Of a potential future window just here
And how the old workers' entrance
Can open up into an airy space
Designed to draw the eye economically
To the front elevation, four floors
Of high ceilings and changing definitions
Of affordable, or if we can present
A case to knock it to dust and built again

How do we recycle words, paradise and mill
In new combinations just familiar enough
To be within decision margins
While still retaining the feel of craft
Of experience moulded just for you

It is not their fault, when it happens
Not directly – the dislocation from the story
Of one young man is not caused by them
The trajectory of a bent nail, hissing
Through a body and on into concrete
Is not their doing, the art on their walls is apolitical
No bloody handprints on the long table
No coded plan concealed in brochures
Between the glossy lines on glossy pages
It isn't their fault, or yours, or mine
None of us is directly at fault in this

They're involved though, direction of travel
When they look at old brickwork
Build thought-towers, see gold in the cracks
Boxed air appreciating as investment
There's a sense of mission over money
Or at least, alongside money, regenerative zeal
Striding purposefully towards a bright horizon
Passionate about our story, genuinely
Sunk up to their wallets in social progress
And seeing extra floors in disused churches
Or beams that bore steaming metal demons
Now cupping cabinets with soft-close doors
Is an act of faith in future and in us
They'd say that, and believe it
But the story is absorbed by them, sold back
To us, and in their vision
Which we then re-absorb, the edges harden
Become less porous with each new version

We believe them and they reflect it back
And the story compacts with each telling
Gets polished to such a hard and brittle shine

And in a small room in the city centre
A young woman unlocks a door
Smells ink, revives a tablet deftly
Reviews appointments, checks progress
Equipment orders, needles, gauze and tape
Thinks of dragons and why it is
That so many people still think of dragons
Spreads magazines a shade more artfully
Enticements on street-facing window ledge
Fanned like invitations to a fictional ball
Checks the height of the chair and bench
Waits for her first client, the start of
A complex Japanese-inflected back-piece
Steels herself for sustained conversation
Puts the kettle on, and does not know
How hard and willingly she'll soon be working

The young man closes his eyes, inhales
Maybe there's a memory here, unbidden
Then reflexively pushed under with a verse
A girl's green eye and a strand of red hair caught just so
Blaze-edged by summer sun against pearl-blue
Or that back-heel into goal, never forgotten
The one he didn't see coming, his body
Twisting in air just so, thoughtless
Applying the right force at the right moment
Inevitably heading for the net, hands on his back
Hands on his head, belonging and celebrated
For an action rooted in such felt rightness
There was never any question of not doing it

The young man opens his eyes, feels need
Of that same unconscious self-positioning
Knowing, he returns to his notes, his books
Needs to prime the soul he feels shrinking
Before the other priming and construction
The final twists of wire, ball-bearing distribution
Chemical balance, violence in stasis
Waiting to slave itself to physics, become inevitable
Memorised lessons to put into practice
And perhaps he thinks of himself as holy
Perhaps not, it doesn't matter, this was
Taught by other men, not God, any God
There is no God in one bare shred of this

Outside the office, outside the young man's room
Outside the tattoo-parlour in the city, the day continues
Long cables snake across arena floors
Lecture halls fill and empty, fill, like tide pools
Mobile phones are fixed, ice clinks in glasses
There is a brief fracas on Oldham Street
The mirrored surfaces of Ancoats trap the sky
Six eggs tumble to their doom in Longsight Asda
The every-twenty-minute tick of London trains
Take their crushingly expensive leave of Piccadilly
Prayer beads click with practised ease through fingers
In Whalley Range, Whitefield and Cheetham Hill
A tour guide marshals tourists to the Lads' Club
While another makes the library dome magic
Engels and Marx are remembered or forgotten
Southern Cemetery is full of dying flowers
An engineer sighs through a too-long drum check
And boys on bikes set out truant across Moston

While, in the triple-insulated office
The street below is just a conversation

Heard two rooms over, shorn of detail
And a flat screen is angled from a wall-bracket
Moving on oiled and soundless bearings
To colour-wash itself to life with aspiration
We will have local artists at the launch event, it says
We will have street food showcasing small producers
We will have modern street-furniture in abundance
Benches that could grace New York or Singapore
Because we believe in this city
And we drive its aspirations, in a way
We see that as our job, to herd it
To tend its growth and fight for its direction
Not haphazardly towards some natural light
But staked, tied lovingly, for global benefit
Teased and encouraged to turn its leaves
To a light they develop out of our mythology

Later that day, warm, spring-pleasant with
Broken clouds, and sun he hasn't noticed
As he bends to his work, half his mind is elsewhere
Feeling the skin of his palm burn bright
In the solid heat of another continent
Resting against a sun-scalded table
As a man in cool shadow navigates
Brisk and clear-headed in his politics
Drawing links in the air with his hands
This verse, this outrage, this outcome
This action to avenge, a spark flying
Arrowing upward from a flame, fire itself
Its harbinger, taking souls with it
One of those souls his, bound for glory
And even then, in that moment he remembered
Trees on night streets, rain in gutters
The mist curling round orange street lamps
He remembered the chill of the evenings

Walking home from friend's houses
Buzzing in his head from smoke and gaming
He remembered sweets sugar dusted on trays
In shop windows, images predating days
When prayer ran like simple lightning through him

These images, though, in that dusty room
Were linked forever to a web of crimes
Like drawing constellations out of lonely stars
And it is this he thinks of, more vivid
Than the evening springtime city around him
This he will think of as he travels through it
Rather than the echo of him in its story
That has faded in his life to almost nothing

He hefts the bag so delicately in the hallway
Like it was a child itself, thinks of
Flashing lights, the bare skin of infants
Slips his arms through straps, rotates his neck
The liquid crack of a bent spine, readied
After a day of such holy concentration
Thinks of every camera that will catch his image
And how little each image caught will matter
Double locks the door behind him
Clicking the tumblers just so, although
He knows they will be battered before long
Bent as the door splinters off its hinges
With the terrible frustration of men
Trying to prevent the thing already happened
He steps into the evening street
He walks through the evening city
The trams move smoothly
The people move smoothly
All the machinery moves smoothly
Blind to his absence from the world they share
And the trains and trams at Victoria Station

Burst their doors with the excited crowds
And tickets are held up for scanners
Seats located, arms raised and lowered
The foyer crackles with anticipation
The great bowl filled with youthful noise
A woman closes her eyes backstage
Stretches, steams her throat, eats fruit
And everything is counting down now
Everything is counting down

The tattooist sits a while after closing
Watches the street, opens a bottle of lager
Lets tension fall out of her in the chair
Where she so often has to reassure
Nervous lovers, or laugh inwardly
As men bite lips to preserve self image
While she paints them with dreams and nightmares
Or half-dreams she has helped them to develop
She kills her beer, texts a friend, waits
With no reply thinks of home, tonight she'll leave it
It's Monday, quiet, save this week for later
Packs her bag, buys bread, heads home
Finds herself in Victoria, lovely glasswork
Rubbing up so oddly against concrete
She always thinks this, waits for the airport tram
Imagines staying on it to the airport, leaving
Watches the crowds stream into the arena
Doesn't think much about them, sees
Two who will die tonight, five of the injured
And doesn't know to this day that she saw them
Gets off at St Werburgh's Road, walks to her flat
Watches TV, gets drunk alone, bath, bed early
Sleeps through it with her phone on silent

The concert starts, it is spectacular
The concert ends, the crowd are happy

The young man wanders thoughtless through the foyer
Stands with his backpack, briefly imagines
A small bird pinned to a vast sky
And –

And I could describe this, but I won't
I could bring language to bear on this
Freeze the moment in words of horror
Name the victims, state their ages
Describe the chemistry, the sound it makes
The effect of the fragments
The sight of the aftermath
I could describe it all in detail, but I won't

Better to concentrate on this
The homeless ran to offer help
The paramedics ran to offer help
The nurses ran to offer help
The surgeons ran to offer help
The parents ran to offer help
The police ran to offer help
The women ran to offer help
The men ran to offer help
The cleaners ran to offer help
The foreigners ran to offer help
The kebab shop workers ran to offer help
The drunks ran to offer help
The developers ran to offer help
The criminals ran to offer help
The shop assistants ran to offer help
The landlords ran to offer help
The sex workers ran to offer help
The religious ran to offer help
The non-believers ran to offer help
The train drivers ran to offer help
The musicians ran to offer help

The designers ran to offer help
The hipsters and the taxi drivers
The boxers and the pilots
The soldiers and the editors
The journalists and students
The secretaries and the t-shirt sellers
The accountants and the ticket touts
The teenagers and grandparents
The city ran towards still present danger
The whole city opened its houses and its flats
People were the best of themselves
This city's people were the best of themselves

And the next day the tens of thousands gather
And they are the best of themselves too
To say love conquers hate, and that is true
And there is a profound silence, Albert Square
Held suspended in a moment of such clarity
Of breathing in before letting go
And the speeches are the story of the city
And that poem is the story of the city too
Ringing out to say – this will not beat us
We will not be made different to each other
If you thought this would make us cower
You have got us badly wrong, so wrong

And then the bees come, in swarms
And that is a good thing too at first
Sluggish after semi-hibernation
They raise themselves from pavements
Unpeel from litter bins, gain dimensions
Shout solidarity, lead to smiling glances
You are in the story too, thanks for showing it
And they mean welcome to strangers
They really do, or we are Manchester
And they mean the heart of this city cannot be shattered

And they mean I will carry this for life

And then the wave rolls on, but we try to recreate it
In seas of flowers and spontaneous collection
Sing Don't Look Back In Anger for the camera
A song where only one line carries meaning
Playing the role now, of togetherness
Performing for the worldwide networks
That flocked more to make content than to help
But maybe part of us wants to be fooled as well

And in that small room in the centre
Plastered with rough-ripped pages
Designs displaying art on skin
A gallery of attempted individuality
A young woman sits, unmarked
Waiting in excitement to be marked
The tattooist stands over her
Holding the needle-piston prepared
With its pigment tank insect-pregnant
Ready to sew together ink and skin
The thousandth bee she's gladly drawn
Undifferentiated liquid primed
For transformation, line of leg
Line of wing and antenna
Line of striped abdomen and thorax
Solidarity and story and politics
The ink-expert flexes her fingers
Bends to the task of piercing flesh
Gives the usual warnings about pain
Not too much, she says, don't worry
And I will always stop if you ask me to
We can pause the story in its making
If something in it is too much to bear
The tattooist asks the woman
Are you from Manchester, knowing

The answer already, would know it
Even if this room was on another continent

And as she does this, a minute's silence ends
In the office high above the city
They are as sad as anyone, these men
Before they carry on their meeting
About where to source the old mine carts to be
Transformed to herb gardens outside a reclaimed mill

The tattooist bends to her task
All the arms, wrists, ankles, backs
Even the single neck she's marked
Blend into one field, one many-hued skin
And she feels warm, she feels good about that
Warm and good and simple to be part of that
Although she hasn't marked herself with this
Or been marked, she understands
After all, her job is that translation
Making real the impulse to commemorate
Lovers' names in copperplate, dead faces
Dylan quotes snaking across indented spines
Politics, within her own strict boundaries
Joking references to fashion and the internet
She knows, but doesn't say, will burn down
To a fading glow of remembrance or regret
The other woman draws breath, tenses
Then relaxes, uses her determination
Wraps her solidarity around her as a comfort
And exhales bravely in the embraced pain

Nobody appears at the window in that moment
To mouth – why are you doing this –
And nor should they, this is absolute, pure
Love and defiance, winged and simple
Placed, to speak from skin for all time

Nobody should ask, why are you doing this
That isn't the question, and anyway
The answer is obvious and true
Because in this moment, this is right
Because in grief and drawing together
This is who we are and how we will get through
And every one of the thousands
Snaking round blocks from tattoo shop doorways
Human canvases stacked needle-willing
Feels this is right and feels the same

But – and even that word feels assaulting
Nevertheless – but – what do we do after?

Because yes they are permanent, etched on us
Yes they are reminders, when the eye catches
But their constancy also helps forgetting
They are made of action, but these bees
Are not themselves an action, lying on us
Just like they lie on pavements, needled
Version of a mouse-click, or a signature
The yellow and black sound of a sigh
Inked clatter of change dropped in a bucket
Insect industry covering a strange silence

We never talk about him do we
We never talk about him as one of our own

So what do we do, after the after?
It can't be as simple as – we carry on
Of course we carry on, never really
Did we have a realistic option not to
Nobody lies in the gutter wailing, sets fire
To institutions, not as many, anyway
As would mean not carrying on

So we carry on, but surely not the same

We don't just take a breath and launch back in
Pick up the story on the beat we left off
Like a raconteur pausing for a dropped glass
At another table, in a crowded restaurant

It seems like this should, maybe, happen
In the midst of keeping close the story
By changing our skin, we change the story
Or at least where we stand when we look at it
Become aware of the space around the pages
What might be in that space, which eyes
Are in the reading room, but unable to make out
The promise and the pride etched in books
Scrawled on walls, printed on t-shirts
Sweetly painful as it is drawn on flesh

Maybe we should look up from the book
Look for those like him, ghosting through the chamber
Connected echoes, not leave the search
To the organised blindness of institutions
Carry it in eye contact, actively aware
Carry it in the act of hello to everyone
Carry it in open eyes that fight the fear-flick
Carry it in asking open questions
Carry it in saying, he was one of ours

These acts will not solve anything themselves
There is no magic dust to banish darkness
But they'll live longer than ink in flesh
Will move more than dead insects do

And anyway, the final act is this
He was ours, not as much as anyone's
But more than anyone's
He was ours, birthed in the same labour ward
And buffeted and buffeting in the same schools

And yes there was a family
And yes there was a religion
But that's true of most of us
He was ours, and the story we tell
Was his as well, was there in front of him
As much as it is written before all of us
He was ours, football and friends
And teenage beer and weed
He was ours in St Peter's Square
He was ours hunching along Cross Street
Hooded and hurrying against the rain
He was ours muttering disapproval
Because the Imam's words were too humane
He was ours that afternoon in Heaton Park
When he went to meet a girl from University
He was ours when he sat outside the library
One Saturday afternoon, waiting for a friend
Looking at new buildings on Moseley Street
Going up fast and hopeful, and beyond
The art gallery school took his class to
Once, although he doesn't remember
Much but one statue and one painting
One disembodied head in the lobby
And a mass of coloured lines
He was ours
Before he lost his path in warmer places
And used the threads we shared
To pull himself back here for mayhem

The story we tell became invisible
Too easily erased to be legible
Against footage of online heroes
Against the steady drop of bombs
Against the slow drip of poison
And old texts, mutant in a new world

And after him, we re-told it, without him
With all those elements, but not the part
Where he was also one of us
His religion doesn't matter, his origin
So much as the knowledge he is one of us
He heard the story, lived it, but somehow
Slipped outside as if he'd never heard it

There will be a memorial to this, of course
I don't know what it should be – how could I?
Probably some permanent rendering of flowers
All I can say is there are different memorials
Names carved on walls, insects on skin
And memorials that live in tiny moments
Flicker in the part of life you can't lay flowers at
Can be carried by the ones who choose the work

If we're going to tell the story
We should at least tell it right
And if we don't, if it can't compete
Becomes invisible against the dark
Then the one who wanders into it
That lightless place lit once and fatally
Is still ours, and was failed
As much by us as by his heritage
Because we are his heritage
More than whatever called him into darkness
And we might have held a hand out
Stronger than the hand that took him